Inside Out

INSIDE OUT

The
Social Meaning of
Mental Retardation

ROBERT BOGDAN AND

STEVEN J. TAYLOR

UNIVERSITY OF TORONTO PRESS

Toronto Buffalo London

© University of Toronto Press 1982
Toronto Buffalo London
Printed in Canada

ISBN 0-8020-2432-7

Canadian Cataloguing in Publication Data

Bogdan, Robert.
  Inside Out
  Bibliography: p.
  ISBN 0-8020-2432-7
  1. Mental deficiency – Social aspects. 2. Mentally
  handicapped – Case studies. I. Taylor, Steven J.,
  1949-   II. Title.
  HV3004.B63   362.3   C81-094740-4

Contents

Foreword

Is it not strange that this may be the first book in which the phenomenology of 'mentally retarded' individuals is given to us by those individuals and not by 'investigators'? As the authors of this volume indicate, this is *not* strange because investigators have always assumed that these individuals could not give us a coherent phenomenology and, besides, how could you trust what they would give you? Drs Bogdan and Taylor teach us otherwise in this volume. One can only hope that the fascinating contents of this volume are harbingers of future studies in which investigators seriously and strenuously try to elicit the phenomenology of people to whom labels have been given – labels that have blinded investigators and harmed those they have sought to help.

This book can be read from numerous perspectives but the one I urge on the reader is one of suspended judgment – forget the labels, our usual preconceptions, and *listen* to the stories. That is to say, read as if the book is an account given by a friend whom you are trying to understand. Inevitably, I assume, the reader will have trouble adopting such a perspective but when he encounters such trouble, he should ask 'why?' The answer will reveal the degree to which we are prisoners of labels with their implicit and explicit meanings.

Reading this book brought back memories from decades ago when my wife and I began to work in a residential institution for the mentally retarded. Neither of us came out of a background in this field and we were relatively ignorant about what these 'children' (that is what they were called in those days) were supposed to be like. We soon found ourselves at odds with how others were seeing the residents. We saw them as being far more complicated and far more interesting than other employees did. Indeed, we saw them – we experienced them – as much more like ourselves than they were different. The present book confirms what we concluded in those early days of our professional lives. As I look back, it seems obvious that we had a decided advantage over others: we had less to unlearn! We were naive in the sense that the authors of this book want the reader to be naive. This is a book not only about certain labeled people but about those who will be reading their accounts.

Seymour B. Sarason
Professor of Psychology
Yale University

Acknowledgments

There are many who contributed to our work. The staff of the Center on Human Policy at Syracuse University provided inspiration. A grant from the Syracuse University Senate Research Fund and the Division of Special Education helped financially. Douglas Biklen, Burton Blatt, Janet Bogdan, Joseph Cunningham, Susan Foster, Andrejs Ozolins, and Harris Sokoloff read and commented on earlier drafts. Our editor, Virgil Duff, did that and more; his prompt and enthusiastic support for our work was important. Margaret Woollard was masterful in her copyediting of the manuscript and made a number of welcome suggestions for improvement. Lois Easterday reviewed the case records cited in the text. Helen Anderson, Jane Frost, and Jovita Legaspi typed the final manuscript. Helen Timmins and Rosemary Alibrandi provided general support for this effort. We are grateful to you all.

Excerpts from Ed Murphy's story were earlier published in *American Psychologist* (Bogdan and Taylor, 1976: 47–52). Sections from the conclusion appeared in *Education and Training of the Mentally Retarded* (Bogdan, 1980). They appear here by permission.

Finally, our thanks to Pattie Burt and Ed Murphy for teaching us about the meaning of mental retardation in our society.

Robert Bogdan and Steven J. Taylor
Syracuse University
Syracuse, New York
1981

Preface

We have vivid memories of our first visits to institutions for the so-called mentally retarded. Our experiences and impressions were remarkably similar. We were taken first to the 'model living units' housing young children with rare conditions and deformed bodies. Amid expensive equipment and busy aides, thirty, perhaps forty, unattended children lay helplessly in seemingly endless rows of cribs. 'Society doesn't want to care for these children,' commented one aide to an observer. 'We do the best we can with what we've got.'

We were also profoundly struck by the wards full of older men and women. There were several coloring books strewn about. A television set encased in wire mesh sat high on one wall. Several of the people were rocking. Most sat quietly, just passing the time. There were no obvious signs of abuse or neglect. Yet the atmosphere was one of boredom and depression, of wasted lives and lost opportunities.

With mixed emotions, we toured the locked units, the institutions' 'back wards.' Our anxiety heightened as we approached the wards for 'severely and profoundly retarded, aggressive, ambulatory, young adult males.' The combined smells of antiseptic and excrement were overpowering. Haunting screams filled the air. An overwhelming desire to flee accompanied the turning of the key to the locked ward door. And there *they* were, an anonymous mass of unwanted humanity. The images are unforgettable: some nude, but most in baggy institutional garb; several in straitjackets or tied to long wooden benches; all with close-cropped hair; many with scars; some hunched over; some drooling. What seemed to be a dozen residents converged on us immediately.

Some of the residents simply wanted to shake hands. A couple hugged us until scolded by attendants. One man began talking about his family and about his brother, who lived at the same institution but whom he had not seen in ten years. He said that he missed his brother and wanted to see him.

Such scenes are common at institutions for the mentally retarded. Indeed, over the past five years alone, we have observed similar scenes at twenty institutions located in eight different states (four eastern, one southern, two western, and one midwestern). In the United States, there are approximately 139,000 people residing in state institutions for the mentally retarded (Scheerenberger, 1979), while in Canada approximately 19,000 live in such facilities (Statistics Canada). The names of these institutions vary. Once referred to as 'asylums' in the United States, these places are variously called 'training schools,' 'state schools,' 'hospitals,' 'developmental centers,' and 'regional centers.' In Canada, they are called 'training centers,' 'regional centers,' and sometimes 'homes.' But these names are euphemisms for dumping grounds at which the most barren conditions and inadequate care may be found. Abuse, drugging, isolation cells, straitjackets, unsanitary conditions, medical neglect, and an utter lack of programming characterize the worst of these institutions, but more subtle forms of neglect may be found at all of them (see Blatt and Kaplan, 1966; Blatt, 1970, 1973; Wolfensberger, 1975; Bogdan and Taylor, 1975; Taylor, 1978; and Blatt et al., 1980). The 'best' institutions are characterized by ennui, impersonality, regimentation, and a lack of privacy.

When we first started visiting these institutions in 1972, we were new to the field of mental retardation. We learned a great deal from those trips and more as we pondered over the questions raised by that first and later visits. Why had those people run to us? Why had we feared them? Why did we assume that they would hurt us? Why were they there? Why did those conditions exist? Why wasn't that man allowed to see his brother? How did these people get where they were? How did they think about themselves? *Did* they think about themselves? What was it like to live in a place like that? What was the meaning of 'mental retardation' in their own minds and in their own lives? What had being labeled 'mentally retarded' done for or to them? What did 'mental retardation' mean in our society? Our training as social scientists eventually led us to frame these questions in broader terms, terms which would help us relate the answers not only to the situation of specific people we had met in these facilities but also to that of all institutionalized people, and in particular to those who have come to be called 'mentally retarded.'

These are difficult questions to answer in social-science terms. They do not lend themselves to traditional social-science research methods, which rely on such things as operationalized variables, questionnaires, and various kinds of statistical procedures. As a result, our search for answers has led us to spend hundreds of hours, over the last few years, talking to residents and former residents of institutions. Some of those we interviewed lived on the very wards that we first visited. Our research strategy was to get to know these people, to get them to feel free with us so that they could share with us as openly as possible their sense of what their lives have been like. We have recorded and studied many of these conversations.

We can begin answering some of our original questions now. For example, we understand that the people who ran to us were starved of attention and affection, and also that they hoped to find, in the touch and the words of a stranger, a break from the boredom of their routine. We also understand better why we reacted with fear. We have come to understand ourselves as carriers of our culture. That is, we have learned and must constantly struggle to unlearn the stereotypes and prejudices surrounding mental retardation in this society. Further, and we consider this point central to our book, we have come to see institutional abuse and neglect as merely an extreme form of the dehumanization and degradation to which the so-called retarded are subjected throughout North America.

In this book, we present the autobiographies of two people who, as one of them indicates, are experts on mental retardation because they have experienced it. Part 1, the Introduction, provides an overview of our own thinking on mental retardation and describes the approaches we used and the details of how these stories were obtained. Part 2 contains the life stories of Ed Murphy and Pattie Burt (both names are pseudonyms),* two former inmates of institutions for the retarded. In Part 3, the Conclusion, we discuss what these stories tell us about mental retardation and compare this work to previous studies on the sociology of mental retardation.

* Names of people, institutions, and places have been changed throughout to safeguard the privacy of all concerned.

1 Introduction

In 1966, Burton Blatt and Fred Kaplan published their now-famous photographic essay on institutions for the 'mentally retarded,' *Christmas in Purgatory* (Blatt and Kaplan, 1966), which depicts atrocious conditions at these facilities.[1] The pictures on which this essay was based were taken with a camera secured to Kaplan's belt and hidden from view by his sports jacket. On one occasion, an inmate of one of the institutions discovered Kaplan's camera and reported it to an administrator whose attention Blatt had monopolized up until that time. The administrator laughed and casually dismissed the report with the remark, 'Boy, these retardates can really have an imagination!'

Ironic, but not surprising or unusual. Those who are labeled 'retarded' have a wide range of imperfections imputed to them in addition to their alleged low intelligence (Lorber, 1974). They are defined as incompetent, irrational, undependable, dangerous, and unable to analyze their lives and current situations. In point of fact, many of the so-called retarded do not possess the imperfections and characteristics that have been attributed to them (Sarason and Doris, 1969, 1979). Many can express themselves and analyze their lives, if we care to listen (Lorber, 1974; Stanovich and Stanovich, 1979). As a society, however, we have chosen not to listen and have long devalued their lives, perspectives, and understandings, as the Blatt and Kaplan example so clearly demonstrates.

In this book we present the life stories, told from their own point of view, of two 'retarded' people: a twenty-seven-year-old man we shall call Ed Murphy and a twenty-year-old woman we have given the name of Pattie Burt. Both have been labeled 'mentally retarded' by their families, school teachers, and others in their lives.

At the age of fifteen, Ed Murphy was placed in a state institution for the 'retarded' (called, for the purposes of this book,

---

1 Blatt has conducted a follow-up study. His findings indicate that conditions in these facilities have changed only superficially (Blatt et al., 1980).

Empire State School), where he lived for four years. After a series of 'family-care' placements subsequent to his release from the institution, he moved to a boarding home which houses, besides himself, four other former residents of state institutions. For the past several years, Ed has worked as a janitor in a large urban nursing home.

Pattie Burt lived in over twenty homes and institutions before being committed to Empire State School. She was ten at the time and she spent approximately six years there. She was later transferred to another state institution for the 'retarded' closer to her original home. She lived there on and off, stayed with a number of families and in other arrangements for periods of time, and eventually moved to a small town where she now lives in her own apartment.

In presenting Ed's and Pattie's stories in their own words, we hope to help the reader experience what life has been like for these people and how they view the world and themselves. But beyond that, these life histories should enable us to understand society better, specifically, to understand the meaning of mental retardation in our culture.[2]

The Meaning of Mental Retardation

'What's in a name?' 'Sticks and stones may break my bones, but names can never hurt me.' While these maxims are part of conventional wisdom, words – labels and names – structure how we think about and act toward others. Labels like 'retarded' have a dramatic effect on those who use them as well as on those to whom they are applied. They direct our attention to specific aspects of designated people. They suggest how we should think

2 Our approach follows in the tradition of the 'Chicago School' of Sociology (see Thomas and Znaniecki, 1927; Angell, 1945; Becker, 1966; Shaw, 1966).

about and treat them as well as provide a justification for action
directed toward them. As we shall see, in the case of the 'retarded,'
names *can* hurt.

The abuses of labeling and the dangers of mislabeling are
acknowledged in the field of mental retardation (Edgerton, 1967;
Edgerton and Edgerton, 1973; Mercer, 1973; Hobbs, 1975). Scholars have debated exactly how many people are retarded and
who should be called retarded. Attention has focused on the so-
called mildly retarded. In his 1967 study, Edgerton described the
stigma experienced by mildly retarded persons and advocated
the creation of a new word to characterize mild mental retardation. Mercer (1973) found that school practices and policies
discriminate against racial and cultural minorities by over-
representing them among the mildly retarded. Braginsky and
Braginsky (1971) characterized mildly retarded institutionalized
children as a 'surplus population' and argued that labeling
exonerates society for putting unwanted children away in ware-
houses. We will have more to say about each of these studies in
our Conclusion. For now, suffice it to say that, although we
share some of the conclusions of these researchers, we believe
that the crucial issue in regard to the concept of mental retardation is *not* that some people (the poor, minority group members)
are falsely labeled, or that the 'mildly retarded' are unfairly
grouped with the severely or profoundly retarded. Rather, we
dispute the efficacy and validity of the concept 'retarded' for any
person, including those with the most profound organic neuro-
logical impairments.[3]

'Mental retardation' is a defective concept – a concept con-
ceived in ignorance at a time when our understanding of human
beings derived from the supernatural. The concept has been so
thoroughly accepted by the expansionist scientists of this cen-

3 Our thinking on this matter is congruent with that of Sarason and Doris
  (1979).

tury that, despite general acknowledgment that there is no adequate definition of the term, it is affirmed that 3 percent of the population is retarded and that retardation compares to cardiac disease and cancer in the extent to which it is a major health problem (Edgerton, 1967). Our research suggests, however, that the concept of mental retardation is not just less than useful, it is actually seriously misleading. The term's scientific aura is deceptive in that it conceals subjective moral and cultural value judgments. This would not matter particularly if mental retardation were not also a demeaning concept which implies a deficiency in the humanity of those tagged. People who are labeled retarded have, upon occasion, been denied due process, forced to undergo sterilization, denied life-saving medical treatment, incarcerated without trial, and subjected to abuses that others without the tag are protected against.

The widespread acceptance of the concept of mental retardation rests on a number of commonsense assumptions on the basis of which both professionals and lay people operate. When queried about their beliefs, professionals often do not state their assumptions outright, but their actions, treatment models, research, and writing reveal their taken-for-granted view. This is not the place to refute these assumptions fully, but our critique of them is important to an understanding of the stories that follow and the conclusions we draw from them.

Is Mental Retardation Real?

What is mental retardation? How do we know if someone is retarded? While professionals disagree on the answers to these questions, most answer them in terms of intelligence quotient (IQ) and so-called adaptive behavior, waiting for the advancement of science to provide precise diagnostic techniques. They believe mental retardation is a condition people have. They do not question that; they only want to improve the ways we have of diagnosing 'it.'

This approach to mental retardation lies at the heart of the matter. As a concept, mental retardation exists in the minds of those who use it as a term to describe the cognitive states of other people. It is a reification – a socially created category which is assumed to have an existence independent of its creators' minds (Berger and Luckmann, 1967). To name something is, in a sense, to create it. Because the objective existence of the condition it is supposed to describe has never been questioned, the phrase 'mental retardation' has become an obstruction to understanding. Rather than pointing to a clear and discrete phenomenon, the concept creates the illusion that disparate and amorphous conditions and behaviors are similar. Like all cliches, it tells more about the people who use the term than it does about the 'condition' it is thought to point to. The phrase 'mental retardation' does point to a state of mind – not the state of mind of the people who are alleged to have it, but the state of mind of those who use the concept in thinking about others. Mental retardation is a misnomer, a myth.

To suggest that mental retardation is not 'real' is not to deny differences among people in terms of intellectual ability. It is to say that the nature and significance of these differences depend on how we view and interpret them. We may distinguish between intellectual characteristics on the one hand, and social definitions and concepts on the other. Just as the existence of people who disturbed or upset others in the Middle Ages did not prove the existence of witchcraft (Szasz, 1970), the existence of people who appear intellectually deficient or incompetent to others does not now prove the existence of 'mental retardation.'

Mental retardation is a crude metaphor (Blatt, 1970; Braginsky and Braginsky, 1971). As Braginsky and Braginsky (1971: 15) write: 'The term mental retardation is simply a metaphor chosen to connote certain assumed qualities of putative, invisible mental processes. More specifically, it is inferred that it appears *as if* retarded mental processes underlie particular behaviors. Or, we infer that behavior appears *as if* it were retarded.' We cannot see mental retardation. Nor can we hear, smell, or touch it. We infer it. In this sense mental retardation is not 'real.' Mental retardation does not exist.

Is Mental Retardation an Absolute Condition?

Mental retardation is thought of as an absolute condition – people are either mentally retarded or they are not. Indeed, the concept of 'pseudo-feeblemindedness' has been used in the mental-retardation field to retain belief in the absolute nature of retardation when professionals have been confronted with people who appeared retarded in some situations but not in others (Kanner, 1948).

Even the smallest reflection, however, suggests that mental retardation is a relative condition (insofar as it can be called a condition at all). The classification of people as mentally retarded depends on organizational and societal values, beliefs, and processes. A person may be mentally retarded at some times or in some situations but not in others. Schools provide the clearest example of how organizations create mentally retarded persons. Through testing and sorting practices, schools classify a large number of children as retarded who function perfectly well at home, in their neighborhoods, and in other situations (Mercer, 1973). For many children, mental retardation is 'primarily a product of the labeling process in formal organizations in the community, especially the Public Schools' (Mercer, 1973: 95). The phrase 'six-hour retarded child' is used to refer to the child who is defined and treated as mentally retarded from 9:00 A.M. to 3:00 P.M. Monday through Friday, but at no other times (President's Committee on Mental Retardation, 1969). Schools define children who do not conform to accepted values and expectations as retarded or handicapped in other ways (see Schrag and Divoky [1975] for a similar discussion of 'hyperactivity' and 'learning disabilities').

The proportion of persons identified as retarded in the general population has increased dramatically over the past century. Prior to the latter part of the 1800s, many who might be called retarded now either blended into the general population or were defined as part of the homeless poor (Rothman, 1971). They were not retarded! As North American society became increasingly industrialized and urbanized and as new waves of immigrants arrived, social changes – the creation of surplus urban labor, mass social problems, crime, delinquency, vice – called forth new definitions, and 'mental retardation' (or 'feeblemindedness' as it was called then) became a salient concept (Sarason and Doris, 1969: 238; Platt, 1969: 36–7).

In urban, industrialized society, the concept of mental retardation provided both a legitimation for the failure of some to succeed and a ready-made explanation for perceived social disorder. Around the turn of the century, early leaders 'discovered' a new class of 'feebleminded' persons and called attention to the presumed menace posed by this class. In 1915, Goddard, well known for his infamous hereditary study of 'feeblemindedness,' *The Kallikak Family* (1912), wrote: 'For many generations we have recognized and pitied the idiot. Of late we have recognized a higher type of defective, the moron, and have discovered that he is a burden; that he is a menace of society and civilization; that he is responsible to a large degree for many, if not all, of our social problems' (Goddard, 1915: 307). Fernald, another leader, offered these thoughts in an address to the Massachusetts Medical School:

The feeble-minded are a parasitic, predatory class, never capable of self-support or of managing their own affairs. The great majority ultimately become public charges in some form. They cause unutterable sorrow at home and are a menace and a danger to the community. Feeble-minded women are almost invariably immoral, and if at large usually become carriers of venereal disease or give birth to children who are as defective as themselves. The feeble-minded woman who marries is twice as prolific as the normal woman ... Every feeble-minded person, especially the high-grade imbecile, is a potential criminal, needing only the proper environment and opportunity for the development and expression of his criminal tendencies. The unrecognized imbecile is a most dangerous element in the community (Fernald, 1912: 90–1)

The development of intelligence tests by Binet and Simon (1916) and Goddard (1910) sparked the identification of the 'unrecognized imbecile' and resulted in an increased classification of persons as mentally retarded (Sarason and Doris, 1969).

Lewis Dexter (1964) illustrates the relative nature of mental retardation in his excellent article 'On the Politics and Sociology of Stupidity in Our Society.' Dexter describes a mythical society in which a major target group of social discrimination is composed of clumsy people, the 'gawkies.' As we value intelligence, Dexter's mythical society values grace. This means, among other things, that the technology of the society is designed in such a way as to require grace for the successful performance of everyday tasks, not because things had to be designed that way, but simply because technologists arranged to have things done that way. Dexter speculates on what would happen to clumsy people in his society. School children would be ranked according to grace quotient (GW). Some would be an embarrassment to teachers and their families and would be sent to special schools and institutions. Clumsy adults and children alike would be social rejects and ridiculed by pantomime jokes. Meanwhile, academicians would write scholarly papers on the 'pseudo-clumsy' and form professional organizations like the National Association on Clumsiness. Dexter even goes so far as to describe the controversy that would surround researchers who concluded that people with subnormal GQ could live independently. The lessons to be learned from Dexter's metaphor seem obvious, yet are often ignored: we, as a society, have created the 'mentally retarded'

through beliefs, values, and practices. The condition is relative,
not absolute.

Is Mental Retardation a Non-arbitrary Classification?

The associated concepts of intelligence and mental retardation
are abstract and imprecise notions (Blumer, 1969). One cannot
directly observe or otherwise experience either intelligence or
mental retardation. Thus, while mental retardation is assumed
to be a pathological condition, there is no specific, identified
physiological or genetic impairment among the vast majority of
persons classified as mentally retarded (Edgerton, 1967; Braginsky and Braginsky, 1971; Mercer, 1973).

Intelligence and mental retardation are concepts operationally
defined by the IQ. IQ and adaptive-behavior scales do not simply
measure mental retardation, they define it. These concepts mean
what testers say they mean. As Sarason and Doris (1969: 54)
note, 'the assessment of intellectual functioning and the diagnosis of mental subnormality are based on conventional tests which
tap a very restricted sample of intellectual functions or processes.'
In addition, IQ tests are developed assuming that intelligence is
normally distributed. Such an assumption assures that a certain
proportion of persons will perform at the lower end of the scale,
not because of their condition or competence but because of the
design of the test.

The artificial nature of intelligence and mental retardation is
illustrated by Canadian geneticist Margaret Thompson's (1964:
15) comment that most people react unfavorably to the state-
ment that 50 percent of Canadians have below-average intelligence.[4] The determination of who is mentally retarded depends
on where we draw the line or set the cut-off point on tests and

4 Incredibly, during World War I, testing of inductees into the U.S. military,
  who were assumed to represent the general population, actually indicated
  that 50 percent were 'feeble-minded' and would never develop mentally
  beyond a 'normal' twelve-year-old (Sarason and Doris, 1969: 295–301).

scales. The cut-off point is arbitrary. Once the line is drawn, however, humanity is divided into two groups – the 'normal' and the 'retarded.' Which you are is based on performance on tests.

Burton Blatt (Blatt et al., 1977) has discussed the arbitrary and changing nature of official definitions of mental retardation. Prior to 1959, professionals generally agreed that the incidence of mental retardation was 3 percent of the general population, with a psychometric 'cut-off' point of 75 IQ or about 1.5 standard deviations from the mean on a normal curve. In 1959, a committee sponsored by the American Association on Mental Deficiency (AAMD) revised the definition of psychometric mental retardation to correspond to a score of one or more standard deviations away from the mean on general intelligence tests (Heber, 1959). According to this definition, 16 percent of the population would be eligible to be designated mentally retarded. In 1973, a subsequent committee of AAMD once more redefined mental retardation to include only those who performed two or more standard deviations away from the mean on intelligence tests; according to this definition only about 2 percent of the general population were retarded (Grossman, 1973). The irony is not lost on Blatt; with a stroke of the pen, he notes, a committee sitting around a conference table enormously reduced the incidence of mental retardation and 'cured' thousands of persons overnight. The classification of people as mentally retarded is arbitrary, resulting largely from an assumption underlying IQ tests and from the level at which the cut-off point is set.

Are the Mentally Retarded a Distinct and Homogeneous Population?

Implicit in the concept of mental retardation is the assumption that the mentally retarded constitute a distinct and homogeneous sub-class of human beings – that their similarities outweigh their differences. In the professional literature, it is common to attribute special emotional states, personality traits, and other characteristics to the retarded (Lorber, 1974). For example, Wechsler (1958: 50), who is famous for the development of one of the most widely used intelligence tests, offered these prejudicial views on the nature of the retarded: 'A mental defective is characterized not only by lack of ability to care for himself but also by an incapacity to use effectively the abilities he does have. His actions are often not only senseless and inadequate but perverse and antisocial as well. He may be not only stupid but vicious.'

The label 'mentally retarded' obscures both the differences among people so labeled and their similarities to those not so labeled (Edgerton and Edgerton, 1973). Labeling entails defining a person in terms of a single dimension and then generalizing about that person's overall character on that narrow basis. There is no evidence that someone with an IQ of 60 has any more in common with someone whose IQ is 20 than with someone whose IQ is 100. Any person – whether 'normal' or 'retarded' – may be talkative or quiet, even-tempered or moody, comical or humorless, affectionate or cold, energetic or listless, short or tall. Apart from their testing performance the 'mentally retarded' do not necessarily have more in common with each other than they do with 'non-retarded' people.

Nevertheless, to be labeled 'retarded' is to be separated from the rest of humanity. The concept interferes with our ability to understand the people so defined as human beings with their own unique qualities and characteristics. Thus, crude stereotypes are substituted for human understanding: 'The mentally retarded don't mind boring jobs.' 'The retarded like to be with their own kind.' 'Mongoloids are good-natured.' 'Trainables are easily frustrated.' By focusing on people's 'retardation,' we lose sight of their humanity.

Is the Concept of Mental Retardation Useful?

Perhaps the strongest indictment of the phrase 'mental retardation' lies not in its logical confusion and conceptual vagueness, but in its devastating effects on people. While mental retardation is assumed to be a neutral, value-free concept, it implies moral inferiority as well as intellectual deficiency. 'Retarded' is a demeaning and stigmatizing label (Edgerton, 1967). To be called retarded is to have one's moral worth and human value called into question. It is to be certified as 'not one of us.'

The terms 'retarded,' 'idiot,' 'imbecile,' and, 'moron' are epithets in general use in our society. 'Moron' jokes pervade everyday conversation. The mass media are filled with derogatory references to people with low intelligence (Bogdan and Biklen, 1977). Newspaper comic-strip characters use 'idiot' and 'stupid' as generic curse words.

If the mentally retarded are not ridiculed, then they are feared or pitied (see Wolfensberger [1975] for a discussion of images of the retarded). Newspapers link crime with mental retardation. For example, one Associated Press release described a murderer as 'an alcoholic and mentally incompetent psychotic who was mentally retarded.' Another newspaper article, captioned 'Mother Kills Tot,' noted that the mother had 'a tenth grade education, most of it in special classes.' Charitable and pitying responses rival the emphasis on criminal tendencies in media portrayal of the retarded. One public-service announcement from the President's Committee on Mental Retardation which appeared widely in U.S. newsmagazines depicted a young child in front of a birthday cake and carried the headline: 'He'll be eight years old the rest of his life.' The message was direct and stereotyped – the retarded are eternally childlike.

These negative stereotypes and prejudiced attitudes are by no means only the misguided views of an ignorant and backward public; such demeaning images of the retarded can be found in the work of scholars and professionals in the field of mental retardation. Public prejudice toward the retarded has its roots in professional myths. Professionals have actively promoted images of the retarded as dangerous, immoral, and subhuman (Wolfensberger, 1975). Indeed, researchers and human-service providers often have been the strongest advocates of forced sterilization, restrictive immigration policies, segregation and institutionalization, and school exclusion (Sarason and Doris, 1969; Wolfensberger, 1975).

Labeling and testing provide a cloak of scientific legitimacy to social control and oppression. The so-called mentally retarded are a surplus population (Farber, 1968; Braginsky and Braginsky, 1971). That is to say, those who are called retarded often do not easily fit into society. They are perceived as deviant, different, and economically unproductive. They represent an embarrassment to others. People diagnosed as retarded on the basis of test scores can be treated in discriminatory ways. As Braginsky and Braginsky (1971: 176) put it: '"mental retardation" is, in fact, a sociopolitical, not a psychological, construct. The myth, perpetuated by a society which refuses to recognize the true nature of its needed social reforms, has successfully camouflaged the politics of diagnosis and incarceration.'

Studies of the effects of labeling and stigma have concentrated solely on the so-called mildly retarded (Edgerton, 1967; Braginsky and Braginsky, 1971; Mercer, 1973). However, the so-called severely and profoundly retarded are harmed as much as, if not more than, the 'mildly retarded' by labeling and related social processes. The phrases 'severely retarded' and 'profoundly retarded' evoke powerful negative images regarding the human potential and moral worth of the people so classified. These persons are thought of and referred to as 'vegetables' and 'subhumans.' For example, Tredgold (1956: 147) described these persons as follows: 'They have eyes, but they see not; ears, but they hear not; they have no consciousness of pleasure or pain; in fact, their mental state is one of entire negation.'

For even the 'severely and profoundly retarded,' social definitions act as a self-fulfilling prophecy (Merton, 1957). Their life chances – how and where they shall live – are structured by people's understanding of mental retardation and the stereotyped reactions the concept brings forth. If we assume that they cannot learn, we will not teach them. If we regard them as subhuman, we will deprive them of their rights. If we regard them as a separate category of human being, we will segregate them and ignore their suffering. The so-called 'severely and profoundly retarded' are victims of the absurd belief that they need less than other people – that a pleasant and decent place to live, meaningful activities, stimulating and challenging tasks, human kindness and affection, and dignity are less necessary to them than to 'normal' people.

The mentally retarded have been abused, dehumanized, stigmatized, and warehoused in impersonal and inhumane institutions (Blatt and Kaplan, 1966; Blatt et al., 1980). Labeling confuses the issue of victims and villains. We blame the wounded for the failings and abuses of society and the service system (Ryan, 1971). When schools fail to teach children, the blame is placed on their retardation. When institutional neglect and deprivation result in 'maladaptive behavior' – for example, rocking and head-banging – it is attributed to the condition of the inmates. Do labels help? Are labels useful? For the persons to whom they are applied – the judged – no.

In this book, we attempt to cast serious doubt on the validity of current concepts and definitions of mental retardation. In so doing, we hope to elevate the discussion of intelligence and mental retardation. The fields of education, rehabilitation, and human services have been engaged in controversies over the relative influence of genetic and environmental factors on intelligence. One side views certain persons and groups as having been born inferior; the other views these same persons and groups as having been made inferior – but inferior they unequivocally are, to both sides. As the debate continues, it is time to introduce a different set of considerations. How do labels and tests affect the lives of people? How do they change the way people think about themselves?

We have yet to hear from those whose lives have been affected by standardized tests and diagnostic categories. The people in this book are such people. They have been tested, diagnosed, and

processed as 'mentally retarded' persons. As their stories suggest, this has had significant consequences for their lives, for
how they think of themselves, and for how others think of them.
What are their IQs? Did IQ tests tap their intelligence? How do
they function in terms of adaptive behavior? What has been the
relative influence of genetic and environmental factors on their
intelligence? At best, these questions seem trite and naive when
held up against the drama of their lives.

The Importance of Autobiographies of the 'Mentally Retarded'

Seldom are those labeled 'retarded' approached with the idea
that they have important insights to offer about their own situations in particular and the field of mental retardation in general.
Instead, the mentally retarded have been studied as a separate
category of human beings. Special theories have been developed
to explain their behavior. This has made it difficult to get to
know those so labeled with any degree of intimacy or depth. The
autobiography of a 'retarded' person is valuable because it brings
us together in a different kind of relationship with a person we
might otherwise casually dismiss as dumb or incoherent or 'not
all there.' The autobiography allows us to get to know retarded
people intimately. It is through this intimacy that what the
retarded have in common with us becomes clear and what is
different about them ceases to dominate how we perceive them.

Reading the autobiography of a 'retarded' person also enables
us to distance ourselves from our prejudices (Becker, 1966). This
distance allows us to empathize with the person – to see the
world from his or her point of view. By freeing ourselves from
our own preconceived notions, we are forced to examine common assumptions about the kind of people who are sharing their
lives with us.

Autobiographies provide a more holistic view of people than
other forms of information do. For example, case records can
give only a very limited insight into people's lives. Individuals

are much more complicated than a profile constructed from a series of IQ tests or from a few pages of selected 'facts' and anecdotes would indicate. Considering a person only from the point of view of his or her official records obscures important things about that person that do not fit the category 'retarded.' Case records emphasize pathological behavior, serving as an indictment of the person rather than presenting a balanced picture of his or her life. The autobiography offsets the limitations of case records by presenting the other side.

The autobiography allows a fuller understanding of the stages in people's lives and the relationships between those stages. Further, the autobiography sensitizes us to the importance of knowing people's past experiences in order to understand the present and the future.

The media through which we view people cannot help but affect how we feel and what we understand about them. Viewing people in terms of aggregate data collected through questionnaires or inventories does little to engender respect for or feelings of closeness to them. Autobiographies foster a respect for the integrity of the individual's experience. They enable us to see people as something more than an aggregate of quantified characteristics.

The author of the autobiography (who is also its subject) has participated in various groups and subcultures which have their own norms, values, and beliefs. The autobiography provides us with an insider's view of these groups and subcultures. We begin to understand the ways in which these groups interact with others and the definitions which arise out of these interactions. While the autobiography cannot and does not provide complete understanding of a subculture, it does provide an initial view of that world through the eyes of an insider.

Similarly, an autobiography lets us see institutions and agencies from the point of view of people who know them as 'clients' (Becker, 1966). By traveling with people who have been 'clients' through their encounters with professionals, we obtain a new perspective on organizations. Through the autobiographies of Ed Murphy and Pattie Burt, it will become clear that clients define professional/client relationships very differently from the way professionals define them. Very often what professionals see as 'treatment' and 'therapy' the client associates with 'boredom,' 'manipulation,' and 'coercion.' From the perspective of the staff, practices such as behavior modification, seclusion, and tranquilizing medications serve a therapeutic end. From the point of view of the 'retarded,' however, they are seen as methods of punishment and behavior control. Autobiographies point up the contradiction between the vocabulary of therapy and the view of the patient, and bring into bold relief the fact that a facility is a far different place for the client than it is for the staff.

Reading the life histories of people labeled retarded thus allows us to understand organizations from the perspective of those who participate in them. In order to develop programs which have the effect one desires, one has to realize that people participating in programs define their own involvement. It is these definitions, rather than the ideas and wishes of program planners, that determine how participants act toward a program. Devaluing the client's perspective by viewing it as naive, unsophisticated, immature, or a symptom of pathology makes many organizations places where one-sided rituals are performed in the name of treatment. The autobiography can help us deal with this problem by educating us with the words of those who know the most about their difficulties.

It is also common for people labeled retarded (as it is for those labeled normal) to be less than candid or straightforward when discussing their lives and feelings. Professionals and others holding powerful positions have rewards and sanctions at their disposal with which to enforce their expectations regarding the client's behavior. The institutional resident who is seeing a counselor knows that he has to 'lay a good story on him' in order to get certain privileges in the institution (see Bogdan, 1974). Thus, clients are pressured to foster impressions consistent with professionals' definitions of appropriate behavior. This presents a very different picture from how professionals would have us view counseling relationships. In good autobiographies, people tell their stories with no holds barred because such sanctions are nonexistent or minimal.

The autobiography reminds us that its narrator has feelings and thoughts that are impossible to study through other forms of research. Such subjectively experienced phenomena as joy, faith, pain, suffering, frustration, hope, and love can be dealt with as they are experienced by real people in the real world, and we can begin to understand what these words mean as defined by people in the context of their lives (Bogdan, 1974).

The 'retarded' individual's own words are the only way we can hear at first hand, unfiltered through the analyses and the understandings of professionals, how life appears to a person so labeled. The autobiography gives an opportunity for 'rebuttal' to people whom we have put into certain categories and to whom we have attributed certain characteristics. In this sense it is a political document in that it provides a platform from which different conceptions of the nature of human behavior can be given force in both the academic and the larger community. Seldom is a forum provided for a confrontation between the client's and the professional's perspective. The autobiography throws into the struggle of diagnosis and theory another voice which encourages us to examine the possibility that we are not doing what we say we are or that we are misrepresenting those we say we are representing. It provides a touchstone, an encounter with reality, that is as important for the health of the relevant professions as it is for the liberation of the clients.

The autobiography is also 'political' in that it serves as a vehicle for the articulation of experiences and feelings that are shared by many others. When read by those with similar experiences, such testimony becomes an instrument for organizing the so-called retarded into a political force. When personal problems rooted in the social structure are articulated, they become public issues and hold the potential for creating social change (Mills, 1959).

The Story of This Project

The autobiographies presented in this book were assembled by us on the basis of in-depth, tape-recorded, unstructured interviews conducted with Ed Murphy and Pattie Burt. We asked open-ended questions, especially in the early stages of the interviewing. While the interviews were guided by our interest in the lives, experiences, and perspectives of people labeled mentally retarded, we did not follow a predetermined interview format.

Edward Murphy and Patricia Burt were not chosen as subjects through a random selection process or any such 'objective' procedure. Rather, they emerged as subjects in the course of other activities. They were chosen because they had special insights into their situations and were articulate spokespersons for the so-called retarded.

When we first met Ed Murphy he worked at a local branch of the Association for Retarded Children. He was recommended as a guest speaker for a course in architecture and social science. Students in the course were being asked to design a living center for the 'retarded' and he was there to tell them what he thought was appropriate for their designs. Ed was engaging and instructive in his presentation. His words revealed that the 'retarded' want the same things that other people want, and that the belief that they need a specially designed facility reflects our own preconceived notions of what the 'retarded' are like. In fact, the word 'retarded' began losing its meaning as he spoke.

We kept in touch with Ed after that experience. Since we were familiar with the institution in which he had lived and the organization where he worked, we had frequent opportunities to talk with him. By contrast with other kinds of social-science interviewing, we knew our 'subject' quite well before the project began.

Approximately two years after we had first met him, we began to consider seriously the idea of working on Ed's life story. We knew that Ed had experienced certain institutions and treatments we were interested in knowing about. We knew he had been declared 'retarded' and we were interested in that concept. We approached him with the idea. Questions about our motives and intentions were discussed, guarantees of anonymity were made, and an overall plan and the logistics of getting started were debated and agreed upon. The fact that our relationship with Ed was almost a partnership set a distinctly untraditional tone for the project.

We met with Ed over a two-year period. During that time we saw him once (and sometimes twice) a week. We usually met at night in an empty office building located in the neighborhood in which Ed lived. Most interview sessions lasted about three hours. The interviews were taped. We tried to create a free and open atmosphere in which Ed was free to express his understandings, hopes, joys, and fears. We attempted to pay careful attention to what he said so as to understand how he ordered and understood his world. If he said things that we did not understand, we assumed that it was the result of a deficiency in our capacity to understand rather than of a deficiency in him. We tried to avoid taking a 'clinical' view of Ed. We did not want to perceive him in terms of preconceived diagnostic categories; rather, we wanted our understanding of his situation to emerge as researchers and subject got to know each other better as people. We tried not to concentrate on the differences between us but rather on what we had in common. We tried to be reflective and to let our own feelings and reactions to what he told us alert us to the prejudices and preconceived notions we carried around as transmitters of our culture. This necessitated our being non-judgmental in our thinking about Ed's experiences and values. We wanted to learn about ourselves as well as to learn about him – or, perhaps more accurately, one of the assumptions of our research strategy was that we could not learn about Ed without learning about ourselves.

We were not completely passive in our interviewing. There were times when we probed in areas that were of interest to us. We sometimes pushed for details when he would have been satisfied with a more superficial description of events. We brought up things that perhaps he wouldn't have talked about if we hadn't asked.

The approach in interviewing Pattie differed from that with Ed only in detail. One of us had struck up a friendship with her when she was a resident at an institution which we will call Cornerstone State School. On visits to the institution, he had been impressed with the perceptive outspoken teenager. When he was told that Pattie wanted to leave the state school but had no place to go, he helped her.

Fifteen months after she moved out, one of the authors approached her with the proposal for the project. During those fifteen months we had seen her occasionally, and spoken with her on the phone. The interviewing started after she had settled in a town approximately one hour's drive from the authors' homes. The idea of the project was first suggested to her over the telephone. The week after that conversation, one of the authors drove down to her apartment, discussed the idea more fully with her, and began recording her story. There were seven three-to-four-hour tape-recorded interviews. Our approach during the tapings was similar to that during the interviews with Ed. Five of the sessions were conducted in Pattie's apartment in Woodard (fictitious name). One was held at one of our offices. The last session took place at the home of a family with whom Pattie had lived near Woodard.

Less time was needed for the interviews with Pattie than for those with Ed for a number of reasons. First, more material could be covered with Pattie in one session. She proved to be much more talkative than Ed. In addition, we had already conducted

interviews with Ed and were better listeners. Also, after Pattie
left her apartment in Woodard, it became more difficult to
arrange to talk to her in private without the worry of being in-
terrupted or overheard. Knowing before the move that this
might be the case, we attempted to cover as many aspects of her
life as possible while she was still living alone. Thus, the discus-
sions contained much less small talk.

In putting the transcripts into their present narrative form we
rearranged and edited the materials and organized them the-
matically. Undeniably, the clarity of Ed's and Pattie's messages
was intensified by this process. However, our goal in editing was
not to misrepresent or cosmeticize either story. We simply combined material in order to provide the fullest description possible, clarified what might be difficult to understand, and deleted
material that was repetitious. What is contained here remains
true to Ed's and Pattie's stories as they were told to us.

When we relate to people labeled mentally retarded, we may
assume that they are not articulate, that they do not have the
ability to think abstractly, that they do not have much to say that
is worth listening to. Clearly, the stories presented here shatter
those stereotypes. They contradict conventional wisdom.

One way the reader might deal with the discrepancy between
stereotypes of the retarded and these autobiographies is to view
Ed and Pattie as exceptions to the rule – to believe that they were
misdiagnosed and are 'not really retarded.' We can assure read-
ers that Ed and Pattie are 'legitimately' members of that group.
They have been diagnosed as retarded by a variety of professionals and have been treated by others as though they were retarded.
According to conventional intelligence tests, Ed's IQ has ranged
from the high 40s to the low 60s, while Pattie's IQ has ranged
from the low 60s to the low 70s. We have met and interviewed a
large number of current and former inmates of institutions for
the retarded who are as articulate and insightful as the two
people whose stories are told here (for others, see Braginsky and
Braginsky, 1971; Dybwad, 1974; Lorber, 1974). We have come to

the point in our own work in the field of mental retardation at which we resolve the contradiction between common stereotypes and the evidence in these stories by discarding the system that classifies people as 'normal' and 'retarded.'

Ed and Pattie are articulate and knowledgeable informants about the social meaning of mental retardation in our society. As with any study, one comes across people who are better able to reflect on and express their experiences and feelings than others. Ed and Pattie are two such persons. But they have much in common with other persons labeled retarded. They have firsthand experience of being labeled 'retarded.' But also, as their stories show, they have perspectives on their lives and situations; they have feelings and emotions; they subjectively experience the world much like anyone else.

2 The Life Histories

Ed Murphy's Story

Chronology

Prologue

There is discrimination against the retarded. There are people out of ignorance who have hurt retarded children. It really doesn't help a person's character the way the system treats you. One thing that's hard is that once you're in it, you can't convince them how smart you are. And you're so weak you can't convince them how smart you are. And you're so weak you can't really fight back. Some of the help you get isn't help. Like the way they talk to you, 'I'll help little Eddie ... you're so nice.' Not that I'm saying that they intentionally treat you that way.

I'm talking like an expert. I had to live it. Shit, I'm just another person out there. I have to pay taxes. I'm not really different. I only had different experiences in my life than you. I can tell you about them. When you are talking about state schools[1] you need experts. Experts are people who have lived it. I'm not taking anything away from scholars who have sat for years in offices and know the problem. But I know the problem too.

Early Life

When I was born the doctors didn't give me six months to live. My mother told them that she could keep me alive, but they didn't believe it. It took a hell of a lot of work, but she showed with love and determination that she could be the mother to a handicapped child. I don't know for fact what I had but they thought it was severe retardation and cerebral palsy. They thought I would never walk.

My first memory is about my grandmother. My grandmother was a fine lady. I went to visit her right before she died. I knew she was sick but I didn't realize that I would never see her again. I was special in my grandmother's eyes. My mother told me that she had a wish – it was that I would walk. I did walk but it wasn't until the age of four. She prayed that she would see that day. My mother told me the story again and again of how, before she died, I was at her place. She was on the opposite side of the room and called, 'Walk to grandma; walk to grandma,' and I did. I don't know if I did as good as I could but I did it. Looking back

---

1 State-run residential facilities for the mentally retarded were referred to as state schools when Ed was growing up and incarcerated. Now they are referred to as developmental centers or regional centers. In earlier times they were called idiot asylums or schools for the feebleminded.

now it makes me feel good. It was frustrating for my parents that I could not walk. It was a great day in everybody's life.

I don't know how old I was when I started talking. It takes time to learn these little things when you're handicapped. It's not easy to learn to tie your shoe. Not to know these little things when you're young and everyone else knows them is hell.

The doctors told my mother that I would be a burden to her. When I was growing up she never let me out of her sight. She was always there with attention. If I yelled she ran right to me. So many children who are handicapped must be in that position – they become so dependent on their mother. Looking back, I don't think she ever stopped protecting me, even when I was capable of being self-sufficient. I remember how hard it was to break away from that. She never really believed, even after I had lived the first six months, that I could be like everybody else. Those early years are kind of blank. My mom was with us most of the time. I remember I had trouble with my arms wanting to go one way and my legs the other.

When I was about seven years old things were out of control. Mom had a nervous breakdown and pa was out of town. My mother's sister took charge of the situation and one thing led to another. It was a very sad experience. The place I was sent to was St Cumming's Home for Children. Joann, my sister, went too. She was on the second floor and I was on the third. I lived in a regular dormitory set-up. We had the old white hospital beds. I don't know for sure how many lived on that floor but there was quite a few. It was clean – I could say that for it – but outside that it was no different from the state school. I was there for a few years – until my parents could get it back together.

Most of the family was behind the idea of us going there – at least the neighbors were. The discussion about what was going to happen to us took place in our dining room. Some neighbors were there. My aunt had gone to them to get all the dirt. Mom didn't have much control. She was there and she gave in. You

32   could sense something was going one – it was in the air. Right after that they told us.

Mom was quite ill, she had let herself go. Dad was out of town so she was alone most of the time and couldn't take the pressure of the kids and all. We were put away first and then my mother was put away. My mother and father had their disagreements but we were only seven and eight so it's hard to remember. I was having problems in school. I have no idea where my mother went but it was a pretty rocky time. My mother's doctors were sold on the fact that she had to be in a state hospital.[2] I learned later that dad had a hell of a time getting her out. The whole thing happened so fast. I remember crying about it. We weren't all that dumb – we knew what was going on. As young as I was, I knew I was being put away.

My family had problems and it was all over the block that I was this kind or that kind of a kid. In school, growing up, it was the same kind of thing. It's very annoying because it follows you around. My mind was slow. I can't deny that. A lot went on when we were kids. We had problems. My mom and dad weren't really ready for us. They got into it over their heads. The family was bogged down.

We did get back together and lived together in our own town for six or so years.

My first school memories was when I was six or seven. I can remember sitting in the classroom, drawing. I can remember the nuns. They were sympathetic – they understood. They served the great Father above so they couldn't knock God's will. I think I was frustrated. I can remember a picture I did – it was a yellow duck. There was blue water in the picture – a yellow sky. Just somehow it stands out in my mind – it was just something about how Sister watched me doing it. She walked over when I was finished and smiled.

2 Mental hospital or psychiatric facility.

Every so often the school had marches with the high school. I remember that I didn't march with them. I tried to a couple of times but I couldn't keep up. I remember this one time on Harrison Avenue when they were marching. This friend of mine and I went up on a porch overlooking the street to watch the parade. I always liked the band music, that's why I remember it. The other kid was there to watch me. I think that it bothered me – not marching – but I don't believe I admitted it to myself. I must have blocked the thought out of why I wasn't there. When my class marched by I was proud of them. I waved and they waved back, but if I had my choice I would have ran off that porch to join them.

In elementary school my mind used to drift a lot. Concentrating was almost impossible. I was so much into my own thoughts – my daydreams – I wasn't really in class. I could make up stories in my head. I would think of the cowboy movies. The rest of the kids would be in class and I would be on the battlefield someplace. The nuns would yell at me to snap out of it, but they were nice. That was my major problem all through school, that I daydreamed. I think all people do that. It wasn't related to retardation. I think a lot of kids do that and are diagnosed as retarded but it's nothing to do with retardation at all. It really has to do with how people deal with the people around them and their situation. I don't think I was bored. I think all the kids were competing to be the honor students but I was never interested in that. I was in my own world – I was happy. I wouldn't recommend it to someone, but daydreaming can be a good thing. I kind of stood in the background – I kind of knew that I was different – I knew that I had a problem, but when you're young you don't think of it as a problem.

A lot of people are like I was. The problem is getting labeled as being something. After that you're not really a person. It's like a sty in your eye – it's noticeable. Like that teacher and the way she looked at me. In the fifth grade – in the fifth grade, my classmates thought I was different and my teacher knew I was different. One day she looked at me and she was on the phone to the office. Her conversation was like this, 'When are you going to transfer him?' This was the phone in the room. I was there; she looked at me and knew I was knowledgeable about what she was saying. Her negative picture of me stood out like a sore thumb. That's the problem with people like me – the schools and teachers find out we have problems, they notice them, and then we are abandoned. That one teacher was very annoyed that I was in her class. She had to put up with me. I was putting her classroom work behind. If I were to do it over again, I think I would try harder to make it in school.

After that I started going to special-education classes for the slow. I still hadn't broken my habit of daydreaming. My lips would move when I did it. I would just sit there. I wasn't paying attention, I guess. It's difficult for me to remember. There are only a few teachers that stick out in my mind.

I also found out I had an eye problem. I had been sitting propped against the blackboard. I wore glasses later on. As the years rolled on I got to understand some things that I didn't understand about myself. I don't think it's fair that a kid should be left not paying attention. To let him do that, and then find out later that there was something wrong. Then to say to the parents that your child is this or that.

I remember one teacher I had when I was a teenager who was great. It was in junior high, I guess, and he really did something for the kids. We did the usual things in class – English, science – but what he did this one year was he took this book about the Middle Ages. It was about killing and fighting – there was a real story to it. We did a chapter each week. We all took part in it and we had to understand what was going on. He made it interesting the way he did it. We enjoyed it.

There were all boys in my special class and my sister was in another. I think that something could have been done for my sister and me. The way it was, we left. I sort of think that I could have gone on to senior high school and gotten a job. They had a job program that was part of the school system. I might not have had to go to the state school.

Like I said, I had this one good special-ed teacher but I can't say the same for some of the others. To be in the field of special education as a teacher you have to do more than take kids on field trips. You have to show the kids that you care. That's a challenge. You have to want to go after the child, to see that the kid comes through. You have to want to see the kid grow up. That's something that you can only share with yourself. These are rewards beyond the reward of becoming a principal. Special education should give a lot of individual attention. There are a lot of kids who aren't in special ed who need the same thing.

One teacher I had did me in. I had one special-ed teacher who didn't want me in her class. That was tragic. I don't think she meant it. She treated me special, but it was heart-breaking to listen to her.

They had this lunch program in school that my sister and I were eligible to take advantage of. I think you paid two cents for milk and got free lunches. I don't know if I liked it. I saw the other kids paying for it, but a hot bowl of soup is a hot bowl of soup.

I found that growing up was hell. We have to change, and there is a lot to growing up. I'm an adult now and there is a lot I missed. When I look at the overall picture, maybe I didn't miss all that much. Going to the high-school prom would have been nice. To have a girl would have been nice. But I just didn't get to do these things. There was a lot of discrimination behind your back. Growing up with other kids is not nice. Kids can be cruel. You don't know what it is like to be made fun of. It's puzzling for a kid.

I was made fun of. I didn't have it as an everyday thing, but it did happen different times. Children can be mean when they want to be mean. You go to school and the minute they know that you're not like they are, they can be after you. In my mind I knew something was different but I never really looked at myself as retarded.

I remember this one time with these two sisters. I was in that teacher's class who was so lousy. These sisters were hell-raisers. They made an ass out of me this one time. They tore my loose-leaf paper. I was over at the religious instructions and after that they dismissed us. They beat me up, calling me things. I was very upset. It was just a thing of pushing me around. They shoved me and pushed me and then started tearing up by books. I don't have to go into it, because it's not even fit to talk about. It wasn't anything they said or did in particular, but I got uptight and started swearing and kicking. I went from one extreme to another. They didn't hurt me, not in the sense of physically hurting me, but they hurt my pride. It got to the point where I remember them holding me back.

The one teacher who didn't like me or my sister – we weren't smart enough for her – we weren't like the rest of the class. She was my teacher when this happened. She had to go to the principal about what had happened the day before. She came into the classroom and complained about me making her late. She made a wise remark to me, 'Oh, I heard about your spectacle yesterday.'

The way the other kids treated you was kind of an invisible meanness. The meanness you have to look carefully to see. I would get pretty upset when I was teased, but then I learned that I had to keep control of myself. It's a lot harder to do that when you are weak. The teasing was one thing, but there was this meanness that you couldn't see easily that kept after you.

I told my mom and dad about some of the things that had happened. What could they do? One of the things that is hard is that you just can't go after people.

I did have this one woman teacher who would talk to me. She was a good teacher. You have to learn things. When I talk about learn, I am talking about what you learn every day. You know, a teacher in special education should not be there to only get you competing in spelling tests. I found growing up was a very slow process. My mind had to go through a lot of changes. It happens to everyone, but for some it's a lot easier than for others.

In January of 1963, without any warning, my father died. A couple months later, ma died too. It was hard on us – my sister and me. We stayed with friends of the family for a while, but then they moved. They told us we had to go. So they sent us to an orphanage for a few months, but eventually we wound up at the state school. I was fifteen then.

Right after my parents died we moved in with the neighbors. It was like a foster placement. We might have been adopted by them. Mom died and there was no one to take care of us so we moved in with them. They were good to Joann and me. They wanted to adopt us. The situation got to the point where we thought we were, and then news got out that we weren't. There were legal hassles. There was money too. There was talk that all they were after was the money. My aunt put that in the air. They were moving up north. They were going to take us, but they moved without us. My aunt sold the furniture. Legally it was our furniture. There was something that should have been done. My aunt didn't like them.

We went to an orphanage then. It was run by the Humane Society. The day we left it was emotional. Everybody was crying and carrying on. I get so pissed off. They could have taken us and saved us a whole lot of trouble. You get so emotional, but it is wasted feelings. We went to the orphanage for three months to get processed.

It was a shame that I had to leave my family and community. I had a dog there that I liked a lot. But I guess you have to be realistic. I mean how ever much I think I wanted it and liked it, it might not have worked out the way you think it would have. People are people and who knows what would have happened to me with my family?

Right before they sent me and my sister to the state school they had six psychologists examine us to determine how intelligent we were. I think that was a waste of time. They asked me things like, 'What comes to mind when I say "dawn"?' – so you say, 'Light.' Things like that. What were tough were putting the puzzles together and the mechanical stuff. They start out very simple and then they build it up and it gets harder and harder.

If you're going to do something with a person's life you don't have to pay all that money to be testing them. I had no place else to go. I mean here I am, pretty intelligent, and here are six psychologists testing me and sending me to the state school. How would you feel if you were examined by all those people and then wound up where I did? A psychologist is supposed to help you. The way they talked to me they must have thought I was fairly intelligent. One of them said, 'You look like a smart young man,' and then I turned up there. I don't think the tests made any difference – they had their minds made up anyway.

Another guy I talked to was a psychiatrist. That was rough. For one thing I was mentally off guard. You're not really prepared for any of it. You don't figure what they're saying and how you're answering it and what it all means; not until the end. When the end came I was a ward of the state.

I remember the psychiatrist well. He was short and middle-aged and had a foreign accent. The first few minutes he asked me how I felt and I replied, 'Pretty good.' Then I fell right into his trap. He asked if I thought people hated me, and I said, 'Yes.' 'Do you think people talk about you behind your back?' And I said, 'Yes.' I started getting hyper-nervous. By then he had the hook in the fish and there was no two ways about it. He realized I was nervous and ended the interview. He was friendly and he fed me the bait. The thing was that it ended so fast. After I got out I realized that I had screwed up. I cried. I was upset. He came on like he wanted honest answers but being honest in that situation doesn't get you anyplace but the state school.

When the psychiatrist interviewed me he had my records in front of him – so he already knew I was mentally retarded. It's the same with everyone. If you are considered mentally retarded there is no way you can win. There is no way they give you a favorable report. They put horses out of misery quicker than they do people. It's a real blow to you being sent to the state school.

I remember the day they took me and my sister. We knew where we were going, but we didn't know anything specific about it. It was scary. My Aunt Mertle had come down. She didn't tell us, 'I'm going to put you away.' It's not good psychology. She came to sign us over to the state, though. They did everything behind your back. I hated my aunt for a long time.

Empire State School

To me there never was a state school. The words 'state school' sound like a place with vocational training or where you get some sort of education. That's just not the way Empire State School is. They have taken millions of dollars and spent them and never rehabilitated who they were supposed to. If you looked at individuals to see what they said they were supposed to do for that person and then what they actually did, you would find that many of them were actually hurt, not helped.

It doesn't do a goddam bit of good putting a person in a place like Empire, but what the hell were they going to do with me? The place was so overcrowded when I got there they couldn't take care of the people they had. Can you imagine a stupid administrator accepting me, saying, 'Oh, we will take him'? I guess they figured: What's the difference with a few more? Who's going to know?

I was a resident in a state school for four or five years. I was about sixteen when I entered. I lived there and I can give you an idea of what it was like. We were pressed for room. When I went there there was over 4,000 inside. There was very little bed space.

I remember the first day at Empire. We drove from East Chester so I got there about 11:30 in the morning. We went to administration and got all the papers and zap, I was in. I think it was a real shady deal as I look back. I watched as they drove away. I saw them get in the car. When I got there I saw a few patients outside working on the grounds. Basically it was shocking. I think that retarded persons are almost allowed no existence. They were exiled from society. It was like prison. You know the reason you were put in prison, though. And you know that at the end of ten years you're out. Going to a state school you're at a disadvantage, though. You don't know what is going on, why you are there, or for how long. The social worker gives the soft hand to calm you.

When I look back, it was a big move. It was hard to live with. At first I sat in my chair all day and thought of the outside. I looked at the outside and the cold walls and the different people. You get scared. You're scared of the big population of people.

I think prisoners have it similar to what I experienced. Basically it's the same thing. The prisoner, if he broke the law, nobody's going to trust him. Somebody said I wasn't right for society and they aren't going to trust me either. The only thing is that I never committed any crime.

Your first day at the institution is an unusual day. It's not like any other day in your whole life. The thing that's so different is, you are different. You're different, the people that you are going to be with are different. Going there makes you feel different. I couldn't describe it, but I do think that. I think I almost knew what I was in store for, but on the other hand I had no idea. I did know about Empire before I went, but I didn't know what it was. When I got to Empire the word 'retarded' was something I had to deal with. I had my own way of thinking about myself – I had my own little world. Looking at it from that point of view, I don't know if I looked at myself from the point of view of me being retarded. I knew I had problems when I went to Empire, but I wasn't sure how I thought about it.

All total, it was nine years that I was a ward of the state. About four I lived in the Empire State School. I stayed in different sections of that place at different times.

First I spent six weeks on the admission ward. It wasn't a complete six weeks because I went over to H Building while I was there. I was in H for two months. You see H is the hospital build-

ing, and I went there because of my hepatitis. In H Building, all of **43**
us that had hepatitis were put in isolation. You just lived among
the people that had the same thing that you had. We did everything together at the same time. There were about ten or twelve
with hepatitis in there at the same time.[4] You couldn't leave
there until they diagnosed you free. Hepatitis is a slow type of
thing to get rid of. In isolation you couldn't go anyplace and
there was no TV.

I had an attack and got sick when I was in isolation at H. I got
really drained right out, we were really sick, vomiting, weakness
in the legs. It took a hell of a lot out of you. Outside of food there
wasn't anything to do all day. The food was different – they
ground it. Grease was not allowed in your diet. The grease upset
me, that was it. I remember one night the doctor on duty came in
to see me – they had to call him. I got sicker than a dog and then I
realized and didn't eat any more.

I remember when I was in H I broke a couple of thermometers;
in fact, I rolled over on one. I fell asleep and they forgot it. The
nurse got quite upset, she told me that she would get hell because
it was broken.

I almost didn't make it. Then the big day came that I went
from H to my first ward. I don't like the word 'vegetable' – but in
my own case I could see that if I had been placed on the low-
grade[5] ward I might have slipped to that. I began feeling myself
slip – they could have made me a vegetable. If I would have let
that place get to me and depress me I would still have been there
today. Actually, it was one man that saved me. They had me
scheduled to go to P–8 – a back ward – when just one man looked
at me. I was a wreck. I had a beard and baggy state clothes on. I
had just arrived at the place. I was trying to understand what
was happening. I was confused. What I looked like was P–8

4 Because of overcrowding and unsanitary conditions, hepatitis is common
  in institutions.
5 'Low grade' is a common institutional term for severely and profoundly
  retarded residents.

material. There was this supervisor, a woman. She came on to the ward and looked right at me and said: 'I have him scheduled for P–8.' An older attendant was there. He looked over at me and said, 'He's too bright for that ward. I think we will keep him' To look at me then I didn't look good. She made a remark under her breath that I looked pretty retarded to her. She saw me looking at her – I looked her square in the eye. She had on a white dress and a cap with three stripes – I can still see them now. She saw me and said, 'Just don't stand there, get to work.'

Of course I didn't know what P–8 was then, but I found out. I visited up there a few times on work detail. That man saved my life. Here was a woman that I had never known who they said was the building supervisor who was looking me over. At that point I'm pretty positive that if I went there I would have fitted in and I would still be there.

Before I went to the new ward, they printed me there. That was weird. They take your fingerprints and then take your picture. I didn't know why they were doing that. It seemed funny at the time. It was just something they did and something they had to have in my file. It could make a person feel like a criminal, couldn't it? That's the part of it that most people don't understand. I don't even think a parent would.

The things that people can tell best are things they've experienced. It's different. It's like sitting and watching the world news and understanding, and being there and understanding. A big problem is when people visit Empire they see what is put in front of them. You don't really see what's what.

There was a lot of fear at Empire. There was fear from each other. Your buddy could be your enemy. If you had a real friend, well, that was something rare. I'm talking about the kind of friend that you could talk to. Mostly the kinds of friends there were where an older man would take a younger kid. The older one would take the younger one and teach him things. It all depended on how good-looking the young kid's body was. I couldn't believe it at first myself, but a younger person became attached to an older person. It happens for the same reasons that it would normally happen. Take a kid who just went in there raw ... green ... he could go run out changed. I know one person who did go the wrong way.

A lot of the kids that wound up at Empire were juvenile delinquents. They were an influence on the place. Not all the guys are delinquents or homosexuals.

Homosexual is a fact of life, I should add. I know people that went through stages of homosexuality. You go through it simply because you are there. You see it and you hear it. You have to grow up. If the experience is there, you take it. A person that is strong can either go one way or the other. That's with being a delinquent, too. At times I had anxiety. But for some reason I resisted. It's hard because it is constant. It's hard to refuse. The young kids they don't really make the choice though.

It's like this, you take a guy in his forties or so, right? He's cool, right? So the guy hits onto a kid he wants to get rid of a load with. Now the kid can either take it two ways. He can just take it or he can have it make him turn into something. I was being pulled down by the weight of what was happening there. I'm over my head talking now. I do know the difference between what's happening and what's happened. It's a very heavy scene. It is very heavy when you get into it. There are too many things to discuss.

When you have the picture of a forty-year-old man – some people thinking about that would even consider it rape. I've seen some of the kids call it rape.

It wasn't all that accepted by everyone. If the word got out – as usual it could damage you too. There is an old-timer there – he could tell when the kids were off and running. You had to learn to ignore those things or you would go nuts. The sad part is that – you know – it's not too much different from the outside.

The way they talk about homosexuality throws me. We have to let the talk out about it. I mean, that is an option just like everything else. I'm talking about tension. You know, it can become a matter of tension. People would say it's wrong but who do we blame for the man being in the shape that he's in – say, at Empire? It's nobody's fault. Even though you're in there and even though you are a part of that, you know individually inside of yourself that 'I'm a man even though I'm inside this place.'

I remember we were walking somewhere with a guard and he said, 'Wouldn't it be nice if the patients could have relations – men and women? It would save a lot on medication.' That was right. They'd feel a hell of a lot better. They wouldn't need all those drugs to calm them down.

If they caught people doing it they had sheets that they would write up on them. Sometimes they would lock them up – put them in isolation or up on the detention ward. Locking them up. Sometimes the attendants would dress residents up with a dress and parade you around the ward. They did these things to guys they would catch naked with each other. 'Bunghole' is what they called it. I never heard that word before I went to Empire. Then they could use the regular punishments. They had these wood blocks they put rags around and you cleaned the floor with them. They could make you clean the johns or take your privileges away. I sort of feel it's pretty stupid. It seems stupid to deny them the thing that they need. If you grow up there at one time in your life it is going to be a part of it. I think women had it harder in an institution. They have to go through the changes of life. And if she's a good-looking kid there's a boy on the boy's side that likes her. These things come out and she has to tackle them. There were some pretty girls at Empire. There were pretty bright kids there too. The girls all had to be supervised. They were locked up a lot.

Some of the patients would shine shoes, to make some money. They got paid different amounts. Some of it was depending on how smart you were. Sometimes they would get paid for what they were worth, but there was no fixed price the way there

should have been. There was Rocky, he was an amazing fella.
There was really only one attendant that really took care of him.
I never got in to the racket of shining shoes but some of them
were screwed and some of them weren't, it depends on if you
were smart. If you were fairly smart and if you had shined an
attendant's shoes or if you shined two or three attendants' shoes,
you could make a deal with them. If you were dumb they'd
screw you if they had a chance. Rocky didn't really do that good.
They would try to get him mad. Like if he washed one of their
cars they would give him a nickel or something. I've seen them
do that. They did that just to shit him. It was the cruelest thing
you could pull on people. They just did it. They just did it to bust
balls. You have to do something if you work there. You could let
this kind of thing get inside of you and after a while it would get
you.

Rocky and I were good friends. If someone gave him a nickel
he wouldn't do nothing. He wasn't a person who could tell the
difference between one coin and another. Even if he knew,
sometimes you had to just keep your mouth shut. They used to
bug Rocky – they would make a fool out of him. Like they would
give him a penny for washing the car. They had these gimmicks
that they used. That's cruel, making an ass out of him. He was
forty years old. Mallow saved Rocky – they were going to send
him to the back ward too. They made fools of the low grades.
They would talk about them. They would discuss things that
would turn your stomach. You can do what you want, but
you're not going to change those people.

I would rather be physically abused than mentally, although I
guess they're both pretty much the same. The mentally abused
can determine how you behave forever, though. If I were seven
years old and went into Empire, I would have lived on D–7. That
was a tough place. That was a strict ward. Discipline right down
the line. I remember going there and seeing the kids with all
their heads on the benches. If they moved, one of those bastard
attendants would come over and slap them. That was cruel.

There was mental and physical cruelty. And then there was the kids being cruel to each other both physically and mentally. I did it. I had to do it to accept Empire. I could never really accept Empire. But the pressures. You had to be cruel to survive. Now you take a person that has been at Empire for thirty years. A lot has happened to them inside.

I was a person who was well-behaved. I didn't make a lot of noise. I wasn't one of those that was locked up all the time or with a sheet tying me down. They could beat you up and while they were doing it be calling you a bastard. Some of the things that happened were so bad I wouldn't even want to describe them. Anyone who didn't go along with the shit they didn't like.

E–8 was the ward used for detention – maximum security. Everyone on that ward was there for disciplinary reasons. To a point there is a need for maximum security. If a person is really violent. Not all people that are retarded are violent by nature. Very few of them are violent. They had a word to use for another discipline – 'candy' was it. That was what they used for the stick that they beat your ass with. They would say, 'Bend over and I'll give you some candy.' My sister, she picked up a lot of the state school lingo. She hung around with the tough ones.

At Empire everybody watched you. There is a belief that practically everybody is watching from the teachers to the attendants to the gardener to the dentist, the Lord knows ... everybody ... You actually believe they have to make reports on what's going on every day. On your general appearance and your general attitude. But you learn to live with it.

Some people were born in Empire. Can you imagine a person being born there and living there? There is a woman there who is a hundred years old.

We got a lot of old Air Force clothing at Empire. There was an air base nearby. They had all the insignias and everything. The general came up or somebody came up and said that they shouldn't have all the insignias on the jackets. Some of the guys had corpo-

rals', colonels', and generals' stripes. They didn't think that was **49**
right. Nobody took off the insignias though.

The clothes weren't good. Let's get down to the nitty-gritty. If
you're going to treat them like human beings you got to give
nice clothes. The state has got the loot. Look what they pay some
of those administrators. They sure got nice clothes. You should
see the way some of them dress.

We had showers in Building 56. A regular hassle. Line up and
take your bath. Then occasionally they'd check you to see if you
had lice or cooties. I never got them. A few of them got that
disease, what is it called? I guess gonorrhea. That wasn't too
uncommon. You got that from someone else. You had to go to
the hospital. That was just the facts of life. Sometimes they
would lie about it and try to get around them knowing. It isn't
bad enough you have to be in that goddam nut house, but you
have to contract all the diseases that mankind don't want. It gets
discouraging. You watch those kids and can feel them.

People that got lice they got it mostly from body odor. They
weren't bathing or the lice they would dive off someone on to
someone else. Oh, God ... I was standing about two feet from a
kid and I jumped back. The goddam thing almost jumped on me.

They had a barber. Some of the barbers really did horrible
jobs. They tore the hell out of your head. I have the scars around
here. But sometimes you would have scars that you got from
fighting or being hit and they'd blame it on the barber.

I wouldn't let people take my picture living in a state school. If I
were sitting there and someone came up to me from the outside
and said I want to take your picture, I would tell them where to go.

Christmas at Empire was pretty much like any other day. You
got clothes for Christmas, though. Things that you needed that
they were going to give you were saved and then given on that
day. They did the best they could. If you had money, you could
buy what you wanted. A lot of packages were mailed in. I got a
shirt one Christmas from home. I still have it. It wasn't torn or

anything. I guess I got it in the summer of around 1964 or '65 as a birthday present. It's a nice shirt – short sleeves. I was an office boy, so I went through all the packages that were coming in. We had packages flooding the place at Christmas. If kids didn't have anything coming in, they would give the clothes. They would wrap them up. The state gave out toothbrushes, combs, and things like that. They didn't go into toys too much.

On Christmas day everybody got up and got around the tree and opened the packages. After you opened your gifts you were thankful. I guess they were thankful and they were happy. Then Christmas dinner came. Turkey was the usual, for Thanksgiving and Christmas. After that you got turkey soup for a while. We all got the day off, too.

I remember one year at Empire. The day after Christmas I had this feeling of violence. There I was in an asylum and another new year was coming. Some of the kids go home for Christmas. They would go home for ten days. After a ten-day vacation they felt pretty fair ... even though they didn't want to come back. It was like they could do it until it was time again, until the next time you went home.

We usually had a Halloween dance. They had a costume contest. They used to have some nice costumes. The people designed them and made them themselves. You could be a bum, an attendant ... a lot of them dressed up in whites. Wearing whites wasn't funny though. Even kids would have rings of keys that they would carry around all the time like the attendants. They kind of looked up to them.

We had dances. That's when they let the boys and girls get together. I danced, I used to get embarrassed though. You can imagine when I went to a party I only danced lousy. Black boys and white girls and white boys and black girls danced. Everyone knew each other. We didn't care about color.

One time we were riding on the bus and a black kid said something about black power. There were six black kids on my ward and the rest white. Now, when someone says 'black power' in that situation, what could happen – right? Well, anyway, some attendant heard about the black power and it shook them up. They got the supervisor all uptight. The black kids were my friends. I stuck up for them, too. I walked right up to the charge[6] – this was a night after they had gone to bed. He respected me, this charge, he knew how smart I was. I said to him, 'Look, what is this, we're making all this noise for six black people. We all enjoy being white, so, let them feel proud. I mean, what the hell.'

That was the only time I remember really getting involved in anything. I never looked at them as black, I guess. They were just my friends.

The first year I was in, I was on the books as going to school but was never actually in a program. There wasn't enough room at the school so I just never went. The first year or so I just worked on the wards. I polished the floor, scrubbed the bathroom, but after a while I did get moved up. I helped move beds. I was a 'working boy.' They were the residents that did the work on the wards like cleaning up and feeding. They usually said 'working boy.' They never said 'men,' but the majority of the workers were men. The majority of retarded people can work, and they can work darn good, I might add. At Empire there were a lot that couldn't read or write but they could labor.

There were other patients that would come over to the ward on H to work. I remember there was this one guy, he wore the old state jacket. He used to come up and watch the ward in the evening. He was an older fellow, much older. The patients would come over to H to feed. There were a lot of guys and they had to change the babies. A lot of times they didn't have enough staff to do the job. Just on H–22 there were a lot to change. I had to change a couple myself. H–22 was a good-sized ward. There were at least seventy on it.

A few times I tried to slip out and not change diapers. There was this one guy I fed, too. It was fast, feeding him. His name

6 The term 'charge' once was commonly used to refer to the supervising attendant on a ward.

was Norman, a small kid. I always did it. I really didn't mind that. It was the diapers that I didn't like. I really liked the little guy. We became quite a team. I changed his diaper, too. He had no control. He was five or six. He couldn't talk but he could smile at you. He got to know me. Around eating time, he would move his head and he'd smile, you know. It was a scary feeling. But, I just liked him. He didn't do anything all day. They were idiotic in that respect. They didn't do anything for him. If there was any hope for him I really don't know.

After ward assignments for a year, I started school. I managed to go to school for a half a day, which wasn't much, but really we sat and did nothing mostly. We didn't get anything academically done. A lot of the kids there, and myself, too, could have learned to read a lot more than we did there. Not living in there as a child, I think I had it much better than most. We talked about our problems. Then in the afternoons I started working at the office. The best job at Empire was building-supervisor's office boy. That was the job I had.

What I did at the office was I went to each ward to get their reports. The whole day had to be written up. Each shift has to be written up and then we take the sheet and take it to file it away. My duties were simple. I was a messenger. The way the place is set up, you can walk from building to building without ever going outside. I went outside on good days because the grounds were nice, especially around the administration building. You passed the girls' side, but we weren't allowed to go anywhere near them. We just went about our business and then came back.

Usually we got up at 6:30 in the morning. I always had a white shirt. The ladies always made sure that I got the white shirt. I had nothing because the state owned all the clothes, but they watched out that I had the shirt. I had a habit of always changing my shirt two times a week. The weekends is when you really got looked at – there were parents coming and anybody could walk in. Then school was open to the public. You always had to be alert.

I can always remember that there was always somebody retiring. Basically, I was a person who did what I was told at Empire. If there was a collection for a Doctor Somebody who was leaving – retiring or something – I would go around with a slip and envelopes and say, 'How much would you like to give to Doctor Somebody's retirement party?' I never looked at the messages that I carried. I couldn't read that well and I figured what was written was none of my business. They made sure to tell me that, too. I did look at things, but pretty diplomatically, nobody ever knew about anything I did. One time I was accused of taking money.

I would hang around the office. But if there was something going on that they didn't want me to hear they would ask me to leave. They never gave me any reasons. You got the feeling that it was annoying to them that we were around and could listen to a conversation. They didn't like it. Of course, a lot of the patients who were office boys used to eavesdrop when the news got hot. They always had a good telegraph line. I was never like that. I did my job. I had to be careful, though. I was asked questions, too. Other patients and staff used to bug me and ask what was going on. I had my own way of handling it. I wasn't going to put my job on the line by leaking things. I said things but didn't tell too much. There were people you knew you could talk to and others who you knew that you couldn't say anything. You had to play it like a game of chess. You had to know who was who.

Another thing about being a messenger was that you represented the building you were in because you had a lot of contact with people. On Sunday you represented the building the most. You were the office boy. I used to get a lot of nice compliments. The visitors were very nice. Not too many people came. It was just family. Only relatives were allowed to come. The office had to be careful in that way. That was 'cause anyone could kidnap a patient out the door and off the grounds. Once some ex-patients took a couple of patients off the grounds. They came in a taxi and took them out.

After my ward duties were done I had it pretty free. I had other work assignments. Others didn't have it so nice. If their work was done they sat around most of the day. The routine was very dull. Very dull. At night we used to watch *Mission Impossible* on TV. We would come down on it like vultures the night it was on. When we would think of how to crack Empire we thought about doing it the way it was on that program. It was really a super program. We were kicking around the idea in joking a couple of times about taking over the place. I could sit down and do a good script for that sometime. A group of us could have sat down and planned something. But with our luck we probably would have gotten caught. Somebody would have bumped into us – or something.

The second good job I had at Empire was in the store. We had three high-school students that were pretty super. They came in to help out on Saturdays and holidays. They came in from the outside and they were good-looking kids. One was called Debbie. My buddy got to like that Debbie. She was a real bombshell. Patients used to love to just sit in the store. Just to look at them and ask them about things. I was paid four dollars every two weeks for working there. That was the only paid job you could get. I have a pair of pants I bought there. I worked there for about two years.

There was a woman from the outside that I liked that worked at the store. That was a groovy store. Well anyway, we got to be real close. She was leaving, anyway, she was going to become a nun. That's what she wanted to do. We all knew that she was going. Up until the time she left, she and I were getting kind of cozy. I don't know what it was, just something that came. The time came for her to leave. Everybody that worked in the kitchen were there in their dirty whites. But I went back to the ward and I got dressed – tie and shirt and everything. Here I was all dressed up so she would know how I felt. She actually shed a few tears.

We worked together two years. I got to like her. Nothing really, nothing really as far as love was. I cried, you know. I never really had that before. I never had to contend with that kind of an emotion before. It was super. I had to get the hell out of there. I was going to drown myself in tears. I still think of her often.

It's funny. You hear so many people talking about IQ. The first time I ever heard the expression was when I was at Empire State School. I didn't know what it was or anything but some people were talking and they brought the subject up. It was on the ward and I went and asked one of the staff what mine was. They told me 49. Forty-nine isn't 50 but I was pretty happy about it. I mean I figured that I wasn't a low grade. I really didn't know what it meant but it sounded pretty high. Hell, I was born in 1948 and 49 didn't seem too bad. Forty-nine didn't sound hopeless. I didn't know anything about the highs or the lows but I knew I was better than most of them.

I Building was a real eye-opening experience. You walk in, you got behind the doors and you saw these people sitting around in nightgowns ... it's foggy ... I can remember looking at everything foggy. Then after that I don't think I was quite the same for a long time. It is really shocking. I don't think I took it too well. The person right off the street would have been knocked right off his feet. I didn't do a hell of a lot at all. I spoke when I was spoken to, but they all seemed to wait. They would smile ... those were the good ones. But then you would hear them screaming and yelling and rocking back and forth. I was there for an hour or so. To be honest with you I wouldn't have walked in there at all if anyone would have told me what I would have walked into. I don't think anyone that was halfway civilized would have walked into there.

The way I got up there was, an employee came over to me when I wasn't doing anything and asked if I wanted to help him. But of course you get used to it. I don't know, you just accept it. They would send people there for discipline to clean the floors.

There is no excuse to have conditions like in I Building. They had plenty of staff. The truth has to be told to the people who work there, too. We have not done this. We have just let them sit around. Most of the people there don't have relatives. The only family they did have gave them up to the state for the simple reason that they couldn't take care of them.

In I Building you could read their faces. I could read how unhappy they were and how unfortunate they were but thank God He puts them in a state of mind so they really don't know where they are. It's hard to tell about what they know. Some of them don't know and then maybe some of them do know ...

People think that those that are worse off, like those on the worse wards at Empire, don't know anything. Most smile, so they had to know. Outside we have to see only appearance. The thing they can't see is what I saw in I Building. We have to assume that the mind is working no matter what it looks like on the outside. We can't just judge by appearance. The people can't see what it is like inside. There is a brain. They know when they are being abused. That is a human being. They have a heart, there is tissue that makes them a human being. They are creatures of God, regardless. If you take away the label they are human beings.

To see somebody with brain damage can be a strange experience if you're not used to it. It doesn't look natural for a person to get up and make all kinds of twitches with their body if you have never lived around it or have never seen it. It is sad to take a child – or an adult, for that matter – and put him into that kind of environment. I don't believe you should confine a person just because he is deformed.

Most people don't know what the word retarded means. When you say the word retarded, people just tend to stand back. There are a lot of different people that fall under the term. In parts of Empire, like this section that I went to, a lot of the individuals were disturbed and deformed. But every one of those people could communicate. They could say, 'Hi' – they knew how to say hi – they knew when I was giving them something. A lot of the people at Empire don't think they are retarded ... not in the same sense that we look at retardation like a mongoloid. That, you can look at it and see it.

When you walk down the street people say to themselves: 'There goes an adult.' When they see a person that they know was in the state school, they say: 'There goes someone retarded.' The struggle that the retarded person has is to realize that he is a human being.

There was lots of neglect on some of the floors. All the shit all over the floor. After a while people who work there just don't see it. To keep up with it would be a full-time job. Just to keep changing those poor people would be a full-time job. The attendants were supposed to do the changing but, let's face it, the residents did it. You adapt yourself to the idea. You know it's not the end of the world. You learn to understand that some are not going to get off the floor and he's not gonna get up and clean himself.

A was the parole ward. People would live there and then go out to work on the outside. There is an awful lot of sad stories associated with that ward. I had a friend that went out to work in a restaurant, and basically the owner turned out to be a slave driver. The state school made the deal. The social worker and you go out and get the jobs. They had you scrub pots, set tables, but you didn't get paid for it. They didn't pay you beans. They made you work hard. The social worker wasn't very popular. Nobody would say anything because they feared the state school. You live there long enough and you're afraid of it. Some guys got big jobs in big places like the fancy motels. It was a good eight hours of dishwashing a day. Most of them washed dishes. Everyone worked hard. One man was quite old and they really wore the hell out of him. There were some horrible aspects of it. They treated you funny.

I was on parole ward for a while. They got me this job at the Air Force base working in the kitchen. They bugged me – locked me in the icebox, scared me half to death. Not paying you was on the QT. I guess the Labor Department got after them. They took terrible advantage of those kids. I don't think that a majority of the people knew how bad it was. State school people are disadvantaged. They work their ass off and don't get anything.

Sometimes He gives you life and then that's all you get. When He doesn't give you intelligence He belts you with something else altogether. We've all been born ... killing would be a sin. One night the attendants killed one of them. What they should have been made to do is to live in it – live in I Building. Take their dignity away from them. If I was working on a ward like that when I knew I couldn't do it any more I'd get out. Working there has to affect you.

I am talking like the people who work at the institution are all bad. A lot of the doctors there are foreigners. It's not their fault. The doctors are degraded by the institution like the residents are. As a doctor you want to do your best. When they first go to a place like Empire State School they try to do their best, but that environment eventually does them in. The state sets them up so they can't do anything. They don't even teach them English. Most of the doctors have families. Most family men will do what they have to to support their family. So they stay and put up with it. They don't have any other place to go. A lot of them aren't certified. Most certified doctors won't work there. The state doesn't pay top dollar so the state gets away cheap.

In a place like Empire there is some satisfaction for doctors. If someone has a sore or something he can put some salve on it but when you're a doctor and you have to sign papers to put people in isolation and you know that the only problem is the place that you're working in, that's rough. It must make them feel like hell. That's not what they are trained for.

I knew one doctor, he was from India, he tried to change the system. This doctor and my supervisor got together and tried to get proper medication. There were arguments over how to properly medicate patients – they didn't want everybody drugged up. The good doctor had some insight about what was in the best interest of the patients. If you're new to a place, like this guy was, and you try to change things, you're telling the other people that the way they are doing it isn't right. Nobody wants to hear that. He left, but it goes to show you that some people try to right wrongs, others just accept what they find.

I was embarrassed going up to a doctor. Everything is on your record, no matter what it is, and they are looking through it. We depend on these institutions and we depend on the professional doctors. They're only people. They can't realize what we go through. You can't blame these people. The time has come to open up the institutions.

A lot of people say that the places can't change or you need a lot of money to change them. Listen, a young person who wanted to could go in there and make changes. He wouldn't necessarily need an awful lot of money. The staff aren't that good. A lot of them come right off the street, if you know what I mean.

I think there are two kinds of people. The kind that does the job because he sees the advantage in it for the people, and the kind that puts up a front. But, why these people get into these professions without having that something ... or maybe they get in and something happens to them.

Some of the patients at the school could be the director, for that matter. They would know the needs of the people more than the people that run it. They hire educated people, but then they are just zoo keepers ... in a human zoo. I'm not saying it's a zoo – they act as if it was.

When you sit down and think about it, what the hell is Empire? What does Empire really represent? Sending someone there is like taking my shoe and throwing it through that window. Look at all the lives that had to go through there and look at the few that actually came up really doing something for their lives.

The whole process is something. First, they intimidate you psychologically. Somebody wants you put there and then these experts analyze you and say, 'Put him in a State School.' They could have set up alternatives so that the kids could be in the community. One big mystery was, who really gave a goddam? Who wants to pick up this kid? And there is no concern from the point of view of the family. If he has a mental handicap or a physical handicap they can make up a big list that looks disgusting. State-school kids have disadvantages. First, being put into the state school is a disadvantage. Not being too intelligent is another one. Going into the state school is like being sucked up a vacuum cleaner. The state takes you over. I'm glad I'm out. Empire was more a mental prison than one with walls around it. Sometimes I would think that I'd get my ass out on the highway and go, but where the hell are you gonna go? I mean, you're in state clothes. When you get down to it, it's like slavery, and the kids would agree.

Living in Empire was not like growing up. You're regimented, like a soldier. You do everything in a line. In the line to eat – if you go to church, you go in a line. Any function you go to, it's in a line.

I remember the day that Bobby Kennedy came. That was something. All day long we knew he was coming, and he walked around. I got a look at him. He told everybody what a snake pit the place was, so it was better for a few days. At least he got some people interested for a while. I really admired that man.

You take a lot of crusaders, though, like local politicians, they go over to the state school and do a lot of yelling. They only do it when someone forces them to, like when someone gets something in the paper about someone being beaten, or is overdosed bad. The newest thing at Empire was someone yelled 'sodomy.' Some parent found out about it and called the legislator. Big deal. If they knew what was going on it wouldn't be that big a deal – one incident of sodomy. Hell, for that matter they ought to

Last week was the first time I went into a state school since I was
discharged as a ward of the state – which makes it about three
years. I just went up to visit. I purposely avoided going there – I
have been nervous about it. There are good memories and bad
memories. The whole idea of having been in a state school makes
you nervous about why you were ever put there is the first place.
I'm out now, but I was on that side of the fence once. It has less
to do with what I am doing than with how the game is played.
Being in a state school or having been in a state school isn't
fashionable and never will be. Deep down you want to avoid the
identification. If I could convince myself that in the end they are
going to be cleaned up I might feel better about it. You have got
to face the enemy, and that's what it is like.

I have come from being a resident of a state school to being on
the other side saying they're no good. It has been brought up to
me – 'Where the hell would you be if it wasn't for the state
school?' That holds water, but now the dam is drying up as I
am on this side. Sure I had a need, but they kind of pitched you
a low pitch. There wasn't anything better. I needed a place to
go, but unfortunately there was no choice of where to go. When
it's all said and done there were those at the school that helped
me, so I'm grateful, but still some other place would have been
better.

You know how a dictator can be put in exile from his country,
well, there is a certain number of people exiled in their own
country – exiled from the rest of society. A prisoner and a person
who is retarded moving into society have the same fears. You
don't know what the hell's going to happen to you when you
walk out there. You have fears about how people are going to
accept you. You wonder how the other people are looking at
you. Those things seem to be petty, but they're not. In the institution things are stripped away from you – and it's quiet. Every-

body tells you what to do. I don't think kids should have so much taken away. They tell you what to do.

Leaving Empire State School

After being at Empire State for four years, it came my time to leave. I had been working toward it but it was hard – hard leaving. They fixed me up with a foster placement in a small village fifty miles from Empire. My social worker, who was a good guy, took me down.

I could have left Empire earlier, but I was not sure. I wasn't going to get stuck on some goddam restaurant job where I would have had to come back to Empire for a rest. The doctor asked me once if I wanted to leave and I said, 'No thank you.' I mean I was happy. I didn't know what was out there, I didn't want to risk it. Actually, my aunt wrote and said I should be leaving. For people getting out it's hard to live. You live twenty years in a place like that – you don't really think there is gonna be a tomorrow, and then you're out. There are a lot of problems with women. How do you conduct yourself in front of a woman, especially if you've been on a ward for years where there aren't any? The amazing thing is once you are out here you are faced with it.

Nobody ever told me I had to work and nobody told me I had to fill out a bank form. If you have never had to face them – wow, it's a brand-new world. That's the only way I can describe it. I lived out before, but only with my mother and sister and family. I never had to work. Never knew what a job was. To be honest with you, I never done a day's labor really.

When you leave a state school, one of the things you really miss is the people. You also find that the world is bigger than you are used to having it. The one thing you find is loneliness. When I first went out and couldn't find work, I spent almost a year just lying around the house. I got quite tired. Some people never lived on the outside and it's rather a shocking experience. Boom, there you are.

Another thing about leaving a place like Empire, you have to resent authority. I think the average person in an institution looks forward to leaving – I know I did – and yet you get scared at the final moment you go to get into the car. You're scared of the challenge of it. There are so many things you have to look forward to. I had some overwhelming visions of what I wanted to do. I always had a thing about sitting behind a desk. I guess that's what I'd like to do. I didn't really look at it – like dish-washing – then you're in a new world. Now I'm mopping floors and I know I won't get many other job offers. I know that I'm better off than most. I couldn't stand eight hours of pushing those dishes around. Yet, I do know guys that do it – it's a job. On the outside you do have opportunities. You can go out and dance. There are a lot of social things that you can do. You can sit and just talk. While it's good, you do have moments. Like to some extent the people down at Empire were my family.

The first place I went after leaving Empire was a family-care home[7] in Plainville. Family care – that may not have necessarily been what I wanted. Family care can be a racket. There are a lot of them that are second-class spots.

I lived at the Browns' in Plainville with a lot of other guys. It was OK for a while, but it didn't work out. I could have stayed there, but the situation was impossible. For one, I was in debt. I owed Mrs Brown money. I have no idea how much it was – maybe a hundred or two. You see, things got out of hand. I had no real clothes, so me, the social worker, and they sat down. I don't know exactly what the agreement was, but they bought me a suit and other clothes out of their own pocket. Come to find out they weren't supposed to do it. There was an agreement that when my funds started coming through, they would get paid back, but I guess that agreement that the social worker made was

7 Family care is a foster-care program for mentally retarded adults and children. A family is reimbursed for room and board for taking people into its
home.

against the regulations, so it didn't mean anything. So to this very day I owe them the money. Mrs Brown holds my guardian – my aunt – responsible. People have a funny way of never bringing up what you owe them, but at the same time always reminding you. It made me feel uncomfortable. Another reason that I felt a decision had to be made about leaving was that they were going to be taking in more state boys. State boys are men from the state school who would just live there and not work. There would just be more trouble. They wanted to get me in the rehabilitation program there, but there are all kinds of formalities to get in the program. You've got to realize that I never worked up to that time – I mean in a real job where you make a mean dollar like I do now.

There was one incidence with old man Brown. One day I came downstairs and I wasn't dressed right. I was going to go to McDonald's. She said to me, 'Go back upstairs and dress right.' I had on beat-up clothes. I said, 'I knew the sentry was going to be at the gate.' The other boys were there. Mr Brown heard that and he said that I had insulted his wife. One of the other residents came up and told me that he was angry and that he was going to come up and give it to me. After that he didn't talk to me – gave me dirty looks.

After that it just wasn't the same – it went downhill. They wrote my aunt a few times about the money. After that we had a few talks and it was decided that it was best that I move on. Somehow money overpowers your vision. The Browns are nice people but there is money to be made. Money rules over sensitivity. The food was good – they treated me halfway decent.

The same thing is happening where I'm living now. There is rumors around that they are going to hike the rent. It's no rumor; he told me last night that it was coming in the near future. It's going to go up to $45 a week. Making the money that the other guys make, they're not going to make it. You can't blame him – inflation hits everybody. It's sad. If you're only a dishwasher like Frank and Walter, how the hell are they going to come up with the money?

I went to a family-care home in Newton after that. I guess it was the best family-care home I went to. The woman who ran the home – Carol Greg – she was a stocky woman. Her mother was out of sight. She's done a lot for the state boys. When you talk about how nice she was, she went out with their Christmas money and bought them new beds. It was the Christmas money sent to them. She saved what money they had and bought them new beds. I don't know if they wanted new beds, but new beds are nice.

I liked Newton. It was a nice little town. It wasn't that nice in the beginning, though. Most people don't know anything about what the word 'retarded' means. The majority don't know – how could they know? The same with the word 'crazy.' The only time they hear the term is when people use to go to talk about some group. If I said that I was going to open up a house tomorrow and put in it people from the state hospital and the state school, people would be up in arms. That's what it was like in Newton.

It was a small village. It wasn't an accepted thing for people from the state school to live there. If it wasn't for the local town minister, the kids wouldn't have been allowed there. It was a nice little town and a lot of nice people there, but they were scared. They didn't understand. They were very uptight. There was this one school teacher that lived next door and she didn't want to see the men sitting around on the front lawn. The minister laid it on the line to her. He said, 'What the hell, people are people, you have to live and let live.' It was accepted. After a while people started calling up the house saying, 'Can I have my lawn raked?' That's how they got to know them. They gave them something for doing that kind of work and gave them some income.

The place in Newton had about the best programs. It wasn't really a question of programs, it was a question of the woman taking a real concern in us. You know we'd go out to places. The thing was, just to take a ride is something. They had a lady come in helping them make valentines. They're grown men in their forties. You know the state school still thinks they're children. I told them that they are grown men. 'Oh no, we're boys.' That was the old philosophy at Empire. 'Boys', see – the older men felt like boys anyway. It was easier to be a boy – let's face it. If you're forty years old, if you can feel like a kid and act like one, if somebody isn't going to throw my age in my face it's all right.

Rather than making valentines, what they needed was to be taken out – even into a field or something – just to get aired out. There were about eight to twelve people at that one place – they called it family care. There were four or five to a room. Some of the guys that were there are up here now.

When I was living in Newton it was nice, but nice is not enough. It was time to leave. I was sitting around. I needed that. I needed to rest up, but I looked at the other men there who were twice my age. I saw them and just knew that I didn't want to be like that. It was like looking into the mirror. There were not jobs in Newton and I wasn't set up there to work. My social worker and I talked it over. I told him, 'This is fine, but there is no doubt in my mind that I could be something else – I want to be a man.' I didn't know what exactly it was to be a man. It was my idea, leaving.

I wanted to work. I wanted to have money. I wanted to start somewhere. I was never crazy about work for work's sake. But I guess I like to work. I don't have to work. I could be taken care of my whole life, but I like to work. Nice is not enough. If you don't have to get up, there is no motivation to get going. You don't have to worry about everything because it is all taken care of. The boredom sets in after you take a good look around you – then nice begins to be questioned. Being nice is not having dignity. You have to worry about respect. Being supported by someone is nice. There is sitting around on a summer day on the beautiful lawn and enjoying that. Being in an institution you are trained to take orders, so you're good at that. It's moving yourself that you have trouble with.

Newton was like my childhood. It's nice to be a child, but in ways it's not nice. You don't have any of the responsibilities when you're a child; everybody does your thinking for you so you don't have to exercise your brain. Freedom isn't something you have to worry about, but for a young person there is not freedom in that environment.

Central City

I was picked up when I arrived in Central City. My social worker came to pick me up. I had only been in that city when I came in for the state fair once. There are two different kinds of social workers as people. There was the kind that came to find out what your situation for the week was. Then there was the kind like the guy who took me to Central City. He had what I would call a young attitude. He was nice and didn't want to restrict you. He wasn't formal – he hung in there. It was tiring – all the moving and talking to all the new people.

When I first moved to Central City, I lived at Mr Strong's family-care home. I lived there about two years before I was discharged from state care. I moved next door to a boarding house which Mr Strong owns where I live now. It's a private home in a regular neighborhood in an older section of town.

Mr Strong – the landlord – he does a great job. He does a real great job for a man his age. Getting us in there and the house operating was their project. They took it upon themselves because they either had to sell the property or do something. Not too many people want big houses, because they're too hard to keep up.

There are ten men living there. We all vary as to different mental handicaps. A lot of the men have handicaps like they can't read or write. The men that live with me are working. They have jobs. Most of them are dishwashers and if they didn't have talent to be able to labor, then they wouldn't be able to survive.

Where I'm living now is very cheap and living is very good. The things I don't like about it is that I am under this mental strain. You work maybe eight hours or nine and you come home and zunk. Then, those who work out at places like Lester's Steak House. There are five or six at the house working out there. They work up until 6:00 in the morning. The guys are on edge because they have worked so hard. They are exhausted and a lot of the men are irritated. You don't have to say much to get a fight going or to get a vulgar word out. It's not uncommon to come home and ask someone to please move and have him give it to you. That's annoying.

We all eat in one place – about eight to a table, sixteen at a time. The cook, he is a good guy. He has had his college education, but because of an accident he had to resort to that kind of work. If he points out something about their dress or manners or something, they get mad. The others will come over and start a conversation and then it gets bigger and louder. The other night I got mad. I said, 'Just quiet down. You've said your piece.' Well, the guy got mad and got up from the table and out the door he went. He feels that there's a big thing about hurting you if he doesn't eat, which didn't bother me. I had already ate, but just sitting there listening to them fight irritates you.

The meals, I might add, are great. He's really quite a cook. But how would you like to be sitting at the breakfast table or the dinner table and hear, 'Bark bark, quack quack?' You can get used to some things. The landlord always yells at this one guy. He must be about forty years old. They yell at him. But this guy really gets bugged – annoying – 'Quack, quack.' He does it just to charge the other guys up. The landlord would give it to him when he caught him.

It's hard. Michael, he's another one. His sister wasn't too happy that they let him go. See, he was discharged. Every so often he throws a tantrum, he gets swearing and the old buzzard, really a crabby old coot. I bumped his arm and he snapped right back – 'Oh, you're telling me.' Oh, you get sick of that.

Also, everybody wants to be cool but nobody wants to take a bath. A lot of them go through Empire and get used to being pushed. They are forced to do everything. When they get out they don't move – there's no pushing. There's a sloppy fella. He walks around like he was in rags. Boy, if I got on a rampage, I'd take all the clothes and burn them. The guy has an old army jacket that he got at Empire. The state school is a sickness they have. You have to fight that. It's a twenty-four-hour thing that is inside you.

I room with two other fellas. We have a lot of petty thievery, but I've been awful lucky. I've never had anything stolen.

My roommate Joey. He doesn't have a job now, but he does some things for my landlord. He painted today – made a buck. My landlord could kick him out because he doesn't have any money. My landlord's good to him. Joey used to work washing dishes. I don't know if he quit or got fired. It had something to do with time. See, there was a snowstorm and they said if he couldn't come in he wouldn't keep his job. And they let him go. I think he's lucky that he isn't working there. He claims he's putting applications in. He doesn't do much during the day. Outside of helping the Strongs, what else can the guy do? He watches TV, he's a good card player, good checkers player. I played with him.

Lou, now, there's one guy that lives with me that has got it bad. Besides not having a job since he's been at the house, the other night he went down and broke the window in the front hall. He's been at a state hospital. He was in prison, too. The guy is really uptight. Recently he wanted to go back – back to the hospital in Southern City. He did work at Lester's once. He just hangs around all day and takes medicine. He busted up a few rooms in another house too. Mr Strong would like to get him back to the hospital, but they won't take him back. Lou was involved in a rape with two others. They got drunk and went after someone. He's been on this rampage so you can't talk to him now.

I don't think I would want to live by myself. If I had a choice, I would have a room where I could have privacy – where I could have a private moment to myself. But also you need a place where you can get together with other people. I've gotten so used to having someone around. Oh, I suppose I strive for it some day, but I don't know. All that loneliness would get to me.

I would say that the majority of the men at my place would like to leave the place and get their own apartments. The younger fellas would, even some of the older fellas. Living expenses and all, it would be tough. I pay $45 a week. If I can stay where I am for a while, I can get on my feet financially. We are still wards of the state and we have a free social life.

The sad thing is that you can't put some lives together. Like the guys that are living down at the Shelter. That's like the Salvation Army. The problem is that places like my landlord runs didn't come early enough for some. Some of the people from the state school needed places to live ten years ago. As far as men and women like my landlord – they have done a good service to humanity. At least, living out from the state school, you can take a walk in the park. You don't have to be very intelligent to take a walk in the park. People like my landlord are special people. They take out their heart and said that these people should have a place to live.

I got a job at the ARC[8] workshop before I moved to Central City. I went from Newton over to the workshop for an interview and then over to my house. I remember, I was five minutes late. A few people interviewed me. They asked me a few questions and gave me a couple tests – speech therapy, mechanical ability, IQ tests. A woman tested me. She showed me some pictures – held them up and asked me what they were. There were pictures of dogs and cats and other things.

I took this test when I was working at the shop that one of the guys told me not to be insulted. They had a square with different

---

8 Association for Retarded Children (now Association for Retarded Citizens in most states). The Canadian Association for the Mentally Retarded – CAMR – is the Canadian counterpart.

pieces and you had to put it together and then they timed you.
Then they asked me to count – count to one hundred.

There were different jobs that I did there. One of them was sorting out different pieces of things from a bucket filled with all different kinds of parts. It got to be so boring you could hardly stand it. I did the sorting day in and day out for a few months, until the contract was over. I got the stub for the first paycheck I ever got which was from the workshop. The check was in my name. I didn't do much saving, mainly spending. I used to go to the Burger Palace a lot for snacks.

I was at the ARC workshop for a couple of years. The ARC then found me a job at a supermarket – taking packages to a car. I only did that for two weeks. It got a little hard on the muscles. It was much better paying than the ARC, but they talked with me and it was obvious that it was too heavy. I liked it. Matter of fact, if I could have done it physically, I might still be there today.

After the supermarket, I got a job at Hilltop Children's Home. It was a place for delinquent kids. They needed someone for being a janitor. The other guy had to leave for some reason. The job was OK, but I didn't get along with the kids. They got after me. They played tricks on me. This one kid got to be too much. I lost my temper on him. You get sick of kids after a while. You have to be a really independent person to work there. I just got in over my head. I worked there from September to January.

I went back to the ARC and worked as a bus aide then – helping them with the kids on the bus in the morning and afternoon. I only did that for a couple months until I got my present job working at City Nursing Home. That was in 1973.

I'm a porter – that's my official title at City Nursing Home. The counselor at the ARC got me the job. We made an appointment and I talked to them. They needed a porter. They were looking for somebody. They didn't just give it to me.

The job I have I can't complain. It's rough. It gets you down, but I've been steady at it. I don't make enough to support a family on, but I earn enough to say I'm employed and self-sufficient.

I get along all right with the other workers. I do my share and they do their share. It usually measures out to be the same. A few months ago I would have said I do more. For a while I was the only porter they had. They couldn't keep anyone on that job. You can't blame them, it is hard work. It is hard work. At times it is very boring. You do it anyway. I vacuum the floors twice a day, take out trash more than three times a day. I walk to work.

There are two others on my shift. One of the others got a raise in pay. Even though I have seniority, I don't feel I need the money. I don't say I wouldn't take the money, but I don't need any more than I'm making now. If I needed it, I would try for a slot in maintenance. I would have to train. I just couldn't walk in on a job in maintenance. You have to be pretty smart. When you're an ex-state-school resident, you have a thing about you.

I don't take care of people. That's not my job. I'm not a floor staff member. I think you have to be really dedicated to take care of people. Some people get bored with that, too. A lot of people there have it bad. I mind my own business. I don't bother anybody and they don't bother me.

There is some talk about unionizing my place. It doesn't make that much difference to me. Now if I were a family man, I might be a little more strong about it. I think that I could get more money. It's rough with a set-up like the union. It's kind of like state schools, a union is good if it does good. But when a group of people get in there and corrupt it then you got trouble. On the other hand, you might get better benefits. I don't feel that I'm being screwed at work. I've had my increases and so forth. I've been treated pretty fair.

I will be working this Christmas at the nursing home. It's not so bad. A nursing home has to run. Those people have to be taken care of. The trash and garbage has to be burnt, the linen collected, regardless of what day it is. I'll get paid for the day.

I take Dilantin for my seizures. It's not really a matter of it **73**
bothering me, because it's something I have to take. That's all
there is to it.

It's been a year since I last had a seizure. There was a time
when I was scared shit about having one. It doesn't bother me
really, now. I do worry about having one when I'm alone. I've
got to be careful about brushing my teeth. The medicine makes
your gums swell.

A seizure is like a short circuit. You just go out. I've been lucky. I
have an inkling beforehand. At first I heard a buzzing in my ears
like the humming of a fluorescent light. Then it increases and then
my focus goes out and then I blank out. I usually fall. Your tongue
goes down your throat. Your muscle in your throat contracts and
your legs kick – the nerve in your leg has spasms. I guess it's like
an LSD trip. I think it's like that in the sense that you have no
memory when you're having it. After you hit the floor you don't
know what is happening. That's the beauty of it. If you were con-
scious of it and you tried to control it, you might kill yourself.

The first seizure I had I was in a diner sitting there with a
friend. I turned around for a fraction of a second when I hit a
flow of warm air. I sensed something. I didn't know what was
happening because I had never had one before. Then the lights
went out. I didn't remember anything until I was home being
undressed. Good thing my friend knew where I lived. My friend
called my landlord and he came and got me. After I have a seizure, I vomit like a madman. You're really sick to your stomach. I
don't understand why that is. My friend didn't know what was
happening. He told me I passed out and he said I vomited. It's
embarrassing because it was in a public place, but you're out
anyway so it doesn't mean that much. I understand it enough to
accept it. After the first one, I didn't go to the doctor or anything.
I wasn't aware that I had a seizure. I had seen people have them
but I didn't know what I had was one.

The next seizure was at the ARC. That time I was taken to the
hospital. I fell on my ass. The lights went out and I collapsed. I hit

my lip and cut it on the way down. I scared the hell out of some people. When I woke up, I was at Central City Medical Center. When I woke up, there were doctors there. I was a sick young man – that was for sure. But again, I didn't know what I had. I woke up and there were some attractive nurses around. I was introduced to my doctor. Right then and there it was explained what had happened. He told me that I had a seizure and a few tests would be had while I was at the hospital. I was there for about a day and a half. After I had my seizure, psychologically I was scared as hell. You're afraid of being alone because if you can't contract your tongue you're finished – you end your career as a humble human being.

There are a lot of people who don't know about it even though there's lots of famous people who are epileptic. After the second one, I knew I was epileptic. I started taking Dilantin then. After that I had two more seizures. Once I had run out of medicine. I was home that time.

I also had one at the nursing home where I work. It was on the second day on the job. I don't know what it was – whether I forgot to take my medicine, or what. I walked out of the dining area into the elevator. I didn't know what to do about it. You have the inkling, but you're not positive. I got as far as the service level and then I blacked out. They took me to the hospital. I went back to work the day after but they wanted a doctor's permission that I was okay to work. I was told to go home until I got it. They took a dim view that I had a seizure on the job. They told me that I worried a lot of people – the night nurse in particular. Good thing she was there. She had a lot of experience with epileptics. She made her point quite well, she was right.

There was a lot of arguments about it. They let me come back to work – but we had an understanding that I was to take my medicine. They said that if I had another one I would lose my job. It was embarrassing because it was only the second day. It scared me that they might let me go. The fact that they needed a porter bad helped me. It was a little tough because you have the

frustrations of the job and then in the back of your mind you
always have the thought that you might have one. I had to work
on thinking positively. I had to work about thinking positively
about the work at the nursing home anyway.

I joined the Boy Scouts in fall of 1971. One evening I was sitting
at home and an employee from the ARC came over and said that
they were starting a Boy Scout troop and how would I like to
join. I said, 'Yes.' Being that I was an adult, I thought they could
use my talents as a leader. They worked hard getting it together
and I know they had several meetings before they approached
me. It's turned out to be a pretty good experience. It's been four
years now. Every troop needs a sponsor and ours was and still is
the Ion club. They are like the Lions club or another civic club.

I gave the president of the Ions an award the year before last. It
was a pin from the council – the Hiawatha Council. It was a big
sit-down dinner and it was the first time I had ever done anything like that. I felt a little strange that night. All I knew was
that I was going to give an award at a dinner. Out of all the guys
in the troop, they selected me to do it. It was at the Hotel Central.
It was a state convention of the Ions so there were a good number of people. I was the only one from the troop. I wasn't at the
main table. We had chicken. I thanked them for the occasion,
thanked the council for having me represent the council. It was a
hell of a nice thing for them to do. The man who asked me sent
me a thank-you letter after and told me to keep the good work
up. I felt pretty cool about it. The papers took my picture giving
him the award, but they never put it in the paper because they
thought I was underage and they thought they might get into a
lawsuit. It made me angry.

At first, personally, considering the kids we had and everything, I didn't think the idea of having a troop would really
work. As far as participation, we have had three outings, and we
have uniforms. We have twenty in the troop and we have only
had two that had to leave. One was put in a special institu-

tion – transferred out of state and the other moved to New York City. We have four patrols now. We have high-school students who are Boy Scouts working with us. I have a troop of five fellas and I am a patrol leader. I also sit in on the planning meetings.

The Boy Scouts is a pretty good organization to be a member of. It teaches you a lot about life. I wish I had joined when I was a kid. It gives the kids a chance to do something. It's one more step toward normalization. When you look at the members we have – two or three clowns. Some of the shy ones have come right along, they are beginning to talk. We have pretty good attendance. We go camping overnight. Mostly we go to Camp Good-works. We try to get the guys cooking over the fire. We haven't had any activities with other troops, but we have a pretty good relationship with the office.

One of these days we hope to get some younger kids into the troop. Mostly we have teenagers. Most of the kids are affiliated with ARC. I am outgrowing it, maybe. I look forward to the meetings. I get a ride over there in our own car pool. The last three presidents of the Ions have been involved with the troop.

I'm on the board of the ARC now. There's thirty-five people on the board. We have good attendance at meetings.

The ARC is good. It gives an education to a lot of kids. The public schools turn them away. They can't do it legally, but they still do. There's always been prejudice and there always will be.

I was nervous when I first started going to ARC meetings. I went once before I was voted in. I was introduced and elected the same night. I was shy because there was an awful lot to understand. People knew my background when I was elected.

I went to a board meeting the other night. I got to the meeting by bus. It was the first time I'd ever taken the bus to there. I've taken it during the day, but I've never taken it during the evening. I usually get a ride to meetings. My ride couldn't go to this meeting.

The discussion at the meeting was to change the title of the organization. I got up to say something. The adrenaline was running through me. I could feel my heart beating. I raised my hand. This is what I was waiting for. I wanted to get that thing changed as quick as I could. I said, 'In my personal opinion I don't like the word "retarded." I don't think that anyone else does. I'd like to see it changed. The kids don't like it. I don't think the other people like it either.' They were taking minutes of the meeting. Here I am making history and they're writing it down. There was a lot of discussion and a lot of questions. Nothing was decided finally.

The word 'retarded' is a word. What it does is put people in a class. I like 'mentally handicapped' better than I like 'mentally retarded.' The other word does sound nicer. It doesn't say 're-tarded.' I mean it doesn't stand out there like thumbing a ride.

This is what I've been living for – to see this changed. Things aren't going to change overnight. They're still going to be called retarded. They're still going to be made fun of. It's a matter of time. There's always going to be people who are going to hold it to the ground. We're on one side of the wall and the stone throwers are on the other.

My day's going to come though. I'm going to straighten those people out. I'm going to tell them the truth. They know the truth. All this petty nonsense.

The guys that live in the house right next to ours are on family care. Their social worker is something. She is always dressed all up – combs her hair up. Gets into this little car and takes off. She takes advantage of them. The day might come when I'll sit her down and tell her – 'Listen, come on, lady, come down and get on the track. Don't use these people like you're using them. I don't like it.' It's her attitude. She comes over to our place and starts talking about the 'boys.' 'How is this one doing?' 'How is that one doing?' and then gets in her little bug and flies away. I don't know anything about the lady except she puts up a good front. I don't know the lady but I'm going to get on her ass one of these days.

That's what's so hard about the system. You look at any part of it and you want to tear it down. I see her walking in and talking to the landlord for a minute and then walking out. She just zips in and zips out. What they have for recreation next door is walking about the block holding hands. Then she brings people in for tours of the place. People from the community and professionals, bringing them in and showing it off. They bring them in here, too. I don't care. I've got my freedom now. I wouldn't care if my place is a pigsty – the thing is, it's my own room. When you're a ward of the state you can't say anything about them coming. I think these guys are free and they have their own lives to live without her interference. I shouldn't be saying anything, because it is none of my business. But to watch this woman go up there, go inside, and do her thing, and then leave like she is going on a social date or something. She doesn't even know these people. I'm waiting – if she comes in here and wants to look at my loft I'll say, 'Get the hell out of here. Take your quack and go, I've had it.' It's bad enough when they own you, that they own your ass and mind. They own body and soul. I just can't wait for the day when they come over to that house. I'm going to be on my toes and I'm going to be cool. If they ask me if they can come into my room, I'll tell them that is none of their business – get the hell out of here. That social worker comes in when they're eating and says, 'Hiya, boys.' She's never used the word 'men.' I think you're either a social *worker* and you work or you're going to be a social worker and be the 'Aw-gee,-that's-touching' type. I can't see these people going into the profession for the glory – 'Oh. I'm helping the retarded.' 'Oh, fantastic.'

The social worker we have is a very nice guy. He's the kind of person that you can sit down and talk to. You can say, 'Well, now I'm ready. What do I do next?' He tries, he's been good in that way. But you have to remember – he is the boss, and he has a boss, and on up the stairs.

Whoever is looking out for my welfare should look at it from the point of view as to what would benefit me.

I think that it's good to be drunk every once in a while. Well, for one thing, everyday pressures can be an awful lot to bear. When you take the average person today, you have a lot of problems. You've got the pressures of work and the everyday living problems. Then there is the possibility that you may not wake up tomorrow. I think that you need to take that few hours and say that I am going to have a good time – not to forget your troubles but to put them aside.

Last night I went drinking with an old friend of mine from Empire. I like listening to music anyway, and that's a good way to get away. I don't like going from bar to bar. We went to a night-club for two shows. I had four beers. My friend said that he spent twenty bucks. The show was better than the last time I was there. There was a lot more music. They did a number from the Fifth Dimension. One from the Four Tops. We went out at about 10:30. It's a pretty dark place, and loud, but we really enjoyed it. If you like to just sit there and relax it's good – can just sit there and get lost. I take a chance going up there with the epilepsy. You can't tell what the alcohol will do.

We left when they started blowing out the candles. The guy I was with drank much more than I did. Drinking is good – you are kind of just out there in space. It was about 2:00 or so when we left. Then we went to a diner for breakfast. We were pretty drunk. We had some eggs and sausage and the place was packed. We got home at 3:00.

I took my first plane trip this weekend – went down to New York City. The first time I was there, too. It was an idea I had in my mind for a long time. You don't get much experience traveling being locked up in an institution for the retarded. I went down with a friend from the house.

The whole procedure – from the cab, to the airport, to the ticket counter, to the being searched – was interesting. I've seen that search thing on TV, but it is interesting to go through it. I heard about plane crashes and everything, but I was along for the trip – for the experience. It's quite a sensation taxiing down the runway. It seems very long till the time you are off the ground. I was sitting there picturing what was going on outside the plane. I had seen planes take off before and I was visualizing what it looks like from the outside. After we landed, we went from the air terminal and got our luggage and got a cab.

We went to the Hilton, but we hadn't made reservations. My friend had $100 and I had $800 in cash so we had enough. The room was OK – $60 a night.

I just wanted to do something different. I hadn't done something different in a while. After lunch we relaxed in our room for a while. They have a TV that you can see movies on. Then we went looking for clothes. We went to John's Clothing Store. We walked in and everything was really moving there. It was really moving all over New York. The salesman took my pal and fitted him in a coat and I just looked around. The salesman was a real salesman. He sold my friend a coat and eventually got to me. I saw this coat and he said try it on. I immediately liked it, not even thinking of another color or anything. The coat was so good I would have taken it without the pants. Immediately I bought the whole thing. The suit was $130 something. I finished it off with shoes and a shirt and a bow tie. I spent $39 for the shoes, and the bow tie – I don't know how much that was. The salesman was a fast kind of operator. He was a good salesman. I don't know if I will ever see a guy like that again. Selling clothes was his business and he was doing it well. He kept moving. 'Try this on.' 'Try that on.' I tried that coat on and I fell in love with it. He said that I looked great in it. I told him, 'I know that.' We told him we were from Central City.

The buildings are so high. You see the superman things. You look up and just see those things climb like your eyes climb up there. After the clothes we came back to the hotel and took a bath and then had dinner in the hotel dining room. We wore our new clothes. The whole trip was so short but so interesting. It was my first time staying in a hotel. There were so many firsts. The ordering of the food and eating all dressed up was all new to me. We had filet mignon. We looked boss. Thinking back, looking at us there, we were something. Dinner for the two of us was $37.

I was taken in by the whole thing. I sat there thinking about how I looked and how important I looked. That living is good for

a weekend. The whole trip was great. But you really have to get
used to living that way.

John's Clothing Store was four blocks from the hotel. That was about the farthest away from the hotel we got. I was kind of scared of getting lost.

While we were in New York, I called my uncle and asked if he would pick us up at the train station in East Haven, which is about a thirty-minute ride. We went to Grand Central Station, and bought our tickets, and got on the train. When we arrived my uncle was there – my mother's sister's husband. We went over to their place for dinner. It was nice to see my relatives. We talked about how I was. We talked about how nice the trip was and everything. Most of it was just a good visit.

I was happy to see my aunt. Even after what she had done in getting me committed. That's in the past. You have got to burn those bridges. We talked a little business. My sister's bills that haven't been paid. The Social Security wouldn't foot the bill for my sister's funeral so there is a bill outstanding. I owe it, kind of, because I am the relative. My aunt claims that she is still getting bills. I could become the executor of the will and could take care of it, but I don't feel like handling that now. She showed me my books.

My aunt and uncle took us to the airport. The airport is like a city itself. We had a hell of a time getting to the gate. We got there a half an hour before time. We got searched again and then we were on our way.

When I started, I said to my friend if we come back with $100 we will be doing OK. And that's just about what we came back with. It was worth it. It took a couple of years to save that. What the hell, you only go around once.

I got to work an hour late the next morning. I did some bragging the next day, and they seemed pretty happy for me. I haven't decided when or where, but there will be another trip.

It's really funny. Sunday I got up and went for a walk. All of a sudden Ann's name came to my mind. She's sort of my girlfriend. I don't know why, but I just thought of her moving in next door to the place where I live. That would be something.

Is there still any magnetism between that woman and me? I haven't seen her in three months, but there is still something, I can tell. We had a good thing going. I opened her up a lot mentally. I saw a very different person there than others see, I saw a woman that could do something with her life. If she could wake up one morning and say to herself, 'I am going to do something with my life,' she could. I don't think that retardation is holding her back so much as emotional problems. If she had confidence that would make the difference. I know she could build herself up.

The family had respect for me, at least to a point, but they don't think she should marry. We got pretty close psychologically and physically – not that I did anything. They don't have programs at the Association for Retarded Children that say to adults you are an adult and you can make it. She has been at the ARC for a long time now. She was a bus aide, so in one way they showed her that she could work; but on the other hand they didn't build her confidence enough to feel that she could go out to work.

The last time I saw her she didn't say a word. When she is pissed off at the world she is pissed off – that's the Irish in her. In my opinion she doesn't belong at the ARC. But one thing is, her parents don't want to take chances. Like a lot of the parents, they send their thirty-year-old kids with Snoopy lunch pails. They are afraid financially, and I can't blame them. If she went out on her own, they are afraid that her Social Security would stop, and then if she could continue they wouldn't have anything – she could lose her benefits.

It is harmful for parents to think of, let's say, a thirty-year-old daughter as, let's say, a six-year-old. The thing is that they don't look at what the future will bring. Say they die and there it is? A six-year-old, someone who thinks they're a six-year-old and has been treated like a six-year-old can't make it out there. Then they go to the institutions. People who are treated like that have a really hard time. They don't get any motivation.

The parents like the thirty-year-olds carrying Snoopy lunch pails. The trouble with the ARC here is that for twenty-five years they have not been preparing the parents to think about their children in a good way.

I first met Ann in 1970. It was when I started working at the ARC workshop. I sat there and maybe the second or third day I glanced over and saw her there. The first time I noticed her was in the eating area – I was having lunch. I looked around and she was the only one there that attracted me – there was just something about her. At first she wasn't that easy to get along with. She put on the cold shoulder and that made me think about her more.

One time I had a fight with one of the boys in the workshop. He was her old boyfriend. This day I was getting off the bus and he said that I pushed him. He pushed me and then when we went to the locker room it got rougher. I yelled at him, 'Get away from me.' I started cursing and we started swinging. I guess he was jealous that Ann was spending so much time talking to me. He was a big guy and he hit me in the mouth and cut it. The staff came and broke it up. They treated it like the whole thing was a joke – they thought it was cute, the two of us fighting over Ann. They ribbed us about it like they always rib about boy and girl-friends.

It took a while for her to understand how she felt. She didn't want to be too friendly. She didn't like me putting my arm around her. We went for walks during lunch and she got pretty fond of me and I got pretty fond of her. One day I asked her, 'Well, how about a movie?' She said, 'All right,' but she had to get her mother's permission. Then one day she said she could go. It was a Saturday-matinee gangster movie. We arranged to meet at the bus stop downtown. I remember that I got down there early and bought the tickets before she came. I met her at the stop and then I went up to the ticket office with the tickets in my hand. I was a little fuzzy – nervous, you might say. Of course you were supposed to give the tickets to the man inside. The ticket woman looked at me – sort of stared and motioned with her finger. It was kind of funny considering our ages. I was twenty-two and she was twenty-eight. It was like teenagers going on our first date.

Being at the state school and all, you never have the chances romantically like you might living on the outside. I guess I was always shy with the opposite sex, even at Empire. We did have dances and I felt that I was good looking, but I was bashful and mostly sat. I was bashful with Ann at the movie. In my mind I felt funny, awkward – I didn't know how to approach her. Should I hug her? You can't hug the hell out of her because you don't know how she would take it. You have all the feeling there, but you don't know what direction to go in. If you put your arm around her she might scream and you're finished. If she doesn't scream you are still finished.

There was a news item today about someone voting in yesterday's election who was a resident in a state school. People were questioning whether that person or the others in that institution should be allowed to vote. The mother of the woman who voted when interviewed said that she didn't know anything about her daughter's voting and as far as she was concerned it was a shame, because her daughter had the sense of a five-year-old and couldn't write her own name. She went to the polls and saw that her daughter had signed the roster and spelled her name wrong and come to find out a social worker had helped her vote. It kind of hits me funny in one way – like, could you picture a presidential candidate coming to a state school campaigning for votes? On the other hand, it only shows us that if people want to vote they should vote – it's a step forward. The only question is, does she legally have the right and does she know what she is doing? The mother doesn't sound like she has much optimism in her daughter.

You take people like me and like that girl that voted. The problem is not that she could or should not vote but that she is in a
state school in the first place.

My sister Joann died at Empire in 1973, right around the time I
started to work at the nursing home. I went to her funeral, but I
don't know what she died of. I'm the only one in the family
living now – ma, pa, Joann, they're all gone.

If I have a day off, or when I am on vacation, I sleep in. Like the
other morning, I slept until 11:00 or 11:30. Your system needs it
to catch up. You just have to get it all off you. Sometimes I get up
and I really don't have any place to go – so I just hang around. I
could go and get a Coke or something, but just hanging in there
is OK. After I have a few days off I am ready to go back. I don't
have any trouble going back – I spring right back to it after I
have been sleeping in.

When I am hanging around, sometimes I look through a book
or two that I have around my place. I was in that literacy-volun-
teers program. The person I used to work with is in the hospital
now.

Transportation is hard – reading is a poor handicap for that.
You take city transit. It's quite simple after you get to know
where you are at. Matter of fact, my first day at the ARC I missed
the bus and ended up walking home. That was quite a night-
mare.

I went downtown today. I went down to go somewhere, but I
never got there. I went around in circles for hours. I walked
down. I went to two different banks – wrong banks. I went to see
a guy about some Social Security business, but I never found
him. I was really pissed. Then his secretary called while I was
out. She was very pissed. I guess they really wanted to find out
what my status is. I'm drawing my father's Social Security, but if
I'm so-called self-sufficient they stop it. I don't care. I went into
two different wrong buildings. Then I went into a garage and got

into an elevator – went up and down. Oh, God. The end of the day was bad. I cleaned my room earlier. That was the best part of the day.

Every so often you feel depressed – you know what I mean? You feel it closing in on you at times. The last few days I've felt it closing in. I got quite boisterous a few times. When the steam is on inside and when I'm under pressure, I yell.

Reflections

I never thought of myself as a retarded individual, but who would want to? I never really had that ugly feeling down deep. You're not knowledgeable about what they are saying behind your back. You get a feeling from people around you – they try to hide it, but their intentions don't work. They say they will do this and that – like they will look out for you. They try to protect you, but you feel sort of guilty. You get the feeling that they love you but that they are looking down at you. You always have that sense of a barrier between you and the ones that love you. By their own admission of protecting you, you have an umbrella over you that tells you that you and they have an understanding that there is something wrong – that there is a barrier.

As I got older, I slowly began to find myself becoming mentally awake. I found myself concentrating – like on the television. A lot of people wonder why I have good grammar – it was because of the television. I was like a tape recorder – what I heard, I memorized. Even when I was ten or twelve I would listen to Huntley and Brinkley. They were my favorites. As the years went by, I understood what they were talking about.

People were amazed at what I knew. People would begin to ask me what I thought about this and that. Like my aunt would always ask me about the news – what my opinions were. I began to know that I was a little brighter than they thought I was. It

became a hobby. I didn't know what it meant, that I had a grasp
on a lot of important things – the race riots, Martin Luther King
in jail – what was really happening was that I was beginning to
find something else instead of just being bored. It was entertain-
ing. I didn't know that that meant anything then. I mean I didn't
know that I would be sitting here telling you all this.

When you're growing up, you don't think of yourself as a person but as a boy. As you get older it works itself out – who you
are deep down, who you ought to be. You have an image of
yourself deep down. You try to sort it all out. What is happening
to it? You know what you are deep inside but those around you
give you a negative picture of yourself. It's that umbrella over
you.

The fact that you have a handicap follows you around. People
don't like the word. We persecute people. The child goes through
everything, and all of a sudden – you're marked with a big 'R.'
By the time you reach the situation you are going to grow into,
there isn't too much difference with what people are going to say
about you.

People tell you you are handicapped in different ways. You're
in a restaurant and you may see people watching you eat and
people make excuses for you. They go over and talk to them.
They say, 'The kid is retarded.' Make an excuse for him. I've seen
that. I've heard them say it, but you love them so you put up
with it. For some reason you put up with it.

It makes me sad to see someone who is forty years old taking a
child's lunch box to work. It almost makes me want to cry. It's
not easy, because parents don't want to let go.

Right now schools discriminate against the retarded. You can
mix handicapped with regular kids, but they won't do it. Parents
of normal kids don't want the retarded kids in their school. I
think if they got the kids in there when they were younger, then
they would grow up being used to each other. The rest of the
world can think of you as retarded, but you don't have to think
of yourself as retarded.

A lot of retarded kids can do the same things that any kid can do. Retarded kids can play the same. If I went to the Boys' Club carnival and they all knew that I was retarded it would have been different. It was best just to be there and swing with the rest. There were the days that I didn't get along with some of them, but that was just like everybody else. That was good for me. It did a lot. If a child – say, a handicapped child – is going to make any progress, is going to grow up at all, you have to bring them out with the public. We are not out of the Dark Ages yet. People are still prejudiced. I blame people who should know better – people who work with the retarded.

I guess IQs are all right if they are taken for some purpose – purpose that helps the person. I saw mine one time. In reality I had a much higher score. I'm a lot smarter. Look at the way I'm talking. It wasn't a question of how intelligent I was. It was a question of how this guy was grading me. I don't think an IQ goes deep enough as far as the individual. It can only score the answers to the questions. It doesn't tell anything about the individual. You don't prepare yourself to get the IQ they give you. If they told you in advance, you could get yourself together. They ask you commonsense questions and you answer, but I don't know they are stupid. They're simple questions like 'What's the first thing that comes to you when I say "dog"?' 'Well, how about "cat"?' And, 'How about the first thing when I say "car"?' 'Well, how about "rat"?' Fantastic, fantastic – roll it right off. The real sad part of it is they are trying to catch you. They're trying to catch what you meant. They have this sheet there with all the answers and then they try to get you, but they don't tell you if you're wrong. The way they give you the test, there is not dignity in it. They simplify it too much. See they say 'dog' and you say 'cat' and you don't know if they want 'horses.'
    Tests really don't tell about the person. This is the real sad part. The guy who is doing the test, you can't really blame him – he's doing a job. He's making a living at it. The sad part of it is he fails, too, because he fails to see I am an individual, a

person. The system fails because it only tells you that we have someone that we have to be responsible for and we send them off. You know, it took them three months to get me to Empire. It's not like they put you in for three years or something. But at a state school, you're just in. You don't realize how far away these places are. It's much easier to get in than it is to get out. You lose so much. They take the human character – you've heard of raping a girl – they rape the character until by the time you get in, you feel so low you don't know what's happening. Then one day you wake up and you say, 'What the fuck am I doing here?' It tears you down.

An IQ – it is simply just another number. Just another filing number. A lot of the people at Empire had low IQs but they weren't low individuals. I worked with guys like Mike Winch. He wasn't low – nothing low about him. He had the only store in the institution. It took three patients to run the store. To keep the institution supplied on weekends in cigarettes and stuff. How low grade could you be and do that?

I haven't had a test for a long time. I don't know how I'd do for sure and yet I can sit still here and chat with you like this. But we all aren't as keen in every area and in every sense. Tests – I don't think they go deep enough as far as the individual goes. Testing is humiliating.

Talking about intelligence. Now I live in a house with other fellas. They've lived the institution life. They didn't know anything. They were freed. They are on their own. If you were to give them an IQ test today, they might be a lot higher. They still might record like they have the mind of maybe a child, but they are still a lot smarter than they were. They have had experiences. They have experienced different things. The IQ test is a fascinating game. It's like rolling dice. Forty-nine isn't what my IQ is. Hell, no. At one time I thought it was, but I think I was brainwashed. I've come back a long way.

The trouble with state-school officials is that they never touch you – they just aren't at your level. I guess that's how the ladder of success goes. You're a person that is put in their care and you're only a number on a sheet. You can hope they are trying to change, but who knows? Those people should have been lifted up, but it's hard. I can understand the frustration of the people who have worked for years and have seen nothing really happen. There is a lot of awareness of the problems, but how to solve them is something else. The word 'retarded' is pretty powerful stuff.

I remember when the governor came to Empire. All the state troopers guarding him, but I never saw him personally. He went to H Building. They had plenty of time to clean the place up, but with some of the places you couldn't do much to clean them up. With the kinds of metal beds all lined up you couldn't hide that. He said that things were great at Empire. What else is he going to say?

What I would like for the governor to give the state-school residents is their right to come and go as long as you don't harm anyone. Be able to go after a worthy trade – maybe learn how to drive a car, build a house. I would like to see people given the kind of school they want. For one thing, they have to be shown respect. When we talk about people who are on the border-line – let's give them all the chances possible. Teach people to make choices. There is no need for things like people being over-drugged. We have to give people maximum chances.

If anyone were really smart, I think we'd open up the doors of Empire and say, 'Look, this is what the problems are. For all these years you've been paying taxes and this is what you've actually been paying for.' Let's let all these windbags go. Everybody would know, and then we wouldn't have to make like we are doing something. What are the problems and how can we serve the people we have to serve? I can't wash the pain of going to Empire away. I think that it is time for people to open up their eyes. It is time to open up those doors.

What is retardation? It's hard to say. I guess it's having problems thinking. Some people think that you can tell if a person is

retarded by looking at them. If you think that way you don't give 	**91**
people the benefit of the doubt. You judge a person by how they
look or how they talk or what the tests show, but you can never
really tell what is inside the person.

Take a couple of friends of mine. Tommy McCan and P.J.
Tommy was a guy who was really nice to be with. You could sit
down with him and have a nice conversation and enjoy yourself.
He was a mongoloid. The trouble was, people couldn't see beyond
that. If he didn't look that way it would have been different, but
there he was locked into what the other people thought he was.
Now P.J. was really something else. I've watched that guy and I
can see in his eyes that he is aware. He knows what's going on.
He can only crawl and he doesn't talk, but you don't know
what's inside. When I was with him and I touched him, I know
that he knows.

It's a struggle. I'll tell you it's a constant struggle as long as I
can remember. You want your brain to function correctly and
you try and try. You're at war with your brain. You want your
brain to function but you have got to watch it. Like the other day
in the cafeteria at work. I took a coffee pot and began walking
out of the dining room with it. I was just walking without thinking. I looked down and there it was. I said to myself, 'What the
hell are you doing?' and turned around and put it back. Your
mind has to keep struggling. You can't give in to that mental-
retardation image. You strive to be extra careful. You struggle to
be not what the image of the retarded is. You can't look the way
they say you are if they call you retarded. Some people can be
real smart, but look and act the way a retarded person is supposed to.

Sometimes being handicapped has its advantages. You can go
slower. Living has always been a struggle to get from the bottom
to the top – trying to keep up with everybody. I could never get
up. There are no short cuts for me – only the hard way. The way I
see it now is that the only thing in life isn't just getting up the pole.

I think I've come a long way, but I've got a way to go. I've
gotten to the point where I can accept certain things. Once in a

while I go out now and I have a good time – I'll do different things. It's hard, though. Like you can't go out and join clubs and things. A lot of ex-residents would like to join the Y. That would be something that I could enjoy. I could go and take a swim. I have to adjust more to a point where I can just relax. I've learned to relax in certain ways, but in others I haven't. I'm still nervous. There are fears for people coming from a place like Empire.

What I am basically trying to say is that for the majority of people a retarded person is someone to be stared at. You don't want to be seen in a public place. It hurts to watch those people being retarded. And don't talk to anyone unless you know who they are. It's rough and you can't take on the whole world. You try to make the best of your situation and try to think that the world maybe is saying, 'He doesn't look all that retarded.' There are people you just can't talk to. They are responsible if they see it and then make fun of it. People are really ignorant. People consider themselves normal and they put a stigma on people who aren't. They do it out of ignorance. I don't expect people to understand the whole problem. I know that handicapped people are people. They feel and they have a lot to give.

It is very hard to go through life with a label. You have to fight constantly. Retarded is just a word. We have to separate individuals from the word. We use words like 'retarded' because of habit – just like going shopping every week and getting up in the morning. The word 'retarded' has to be there if you are going to give people help, but what the hell is the sense of calling someone retarded and not giving them anything?

I don't know. Maybe I used to be retarded. That's what they said anyway. I wish they could see me now. I wonder what they'd say if they could see me holding down a regular job and doing all kinds of things. I bet they wouldn't believe it.

Pattie Burt's Story

Chronology

The First Years

I was born in Central City, January 27, 1955. My mother said that I was a fat, plumpy baby. I weighed nine pounds and twelve ounces. I had blue eyes and a lot of goldenlock hair. My mom and dad were taking care of six children. Mom had some other ones but two of them were put out in foster homes. One of those was out of wedlock. All of us that were at home were not all from the same father.

Dad was a heavy drinker. I know it now. My mom told me that that was one thing that caused them to break up. Dad never really let us sit on his lap. When I was two years old, my mom would be cooking and she would say to him, 'Will you please hold her till I get done?' He would say, 'No.' He would push us away. My mom would take us and put us in the playpen. His paper was more important than his children.

He used to beat us. My mom told me when I was a baby, dad came home drunk and picked me up and threw me into the other room. Just picked me up and threw me. My mom went almost berserk on him and almost stabbed him because she was so upset. She said she told him that that would be the last time he'd do that. He wet on my sister too. He was drunk. Got her all soaked. Mom told him if he couldn't act right, he better stay out. Father got mad at her, took her and turned her upside down in the playpen. She got right back up and she shook her fists and told him that if he did that again he would be out of the house for good. Mom and dad were just on pins and needles all the time. They got divorced, but we didn't know that for a while.

Mom told me that one day she said to my father, 'I think that it would be a good idea if we would split the kids up. They need a better home. They need better care and we can't give it to them. There is too many people and not enough money to go around. You come home drunk and do bad things to the children. It isn't fair.' So my mom found out from the welfare what they could do with us and they found us a foster home. I don't think those were the only reasons my mom put us away. She was a drinker and she ran around and stuff.

So anyways, two of us went into foster homes. My sister was four and I was two. I don't remember anything – who the names were, where we lived, or anything. We could have lived in another state for all I know. We were in twenty-one different foster homes from when I was two till when I was seven. The last one, where I was seven years old, was Mr and Mrs Mills in Pen-

rose, New York. They lived out in the country and we had a big
farm house with a dog and some pigs and horses and a garden
and everything like that. They were nice at the beginning because
they were getting money for us through the county welfare – that
changed.

They put me in school. I was seven years old and needed to get
to school. I didn't really learn too much. I did more fooling
around and playing than anything. I put tacks on teachers'
chairs and ran up and down the halls screaming and hollering
and pulling people's hair and knocking them over and stuff like
that. A lot of times in the cafeteria I would throw food and stuff
just to fool around. This is when I was seven – the first year I
went to school. I thought it was a ball. My teacher would get
after me and send me to the principal's office. School was just
one thing I could never get attached to. I didn't like it for some
reason. I don't know why it was; maybe because there was too
many kids or too many bossy teachers or too much disturbance. I
was a bad girl.

The only thing I could think of why I was acting that way in
school was because I knew I had a mom and that my foster parents were not my mother and father. I knew that because of the
way they treated me and she told me, 'Look – you are my foster
child, these are my children here.' She phrased it to me like that,
so I knew that she was not my mom. I was pretty sad. I would
come home and look forward to having a phone call from my
mom or something saying that she was coming to visit. Sometimes she did come, not very frequently, though. Very, very
seldom – but she came.

The Mills had three or four kids of their own and then me. I
remember one time I came home from school with a bad report
with a note that the teacher had put in my pocket. I always had
somebody pick me up right in front of the school where all the
buses line up. I think it was a counselor. She took me home
because my foster parents were working or something. Well,
anyways, I came home with that note. I didn't want to show it to

her. I wasn't going to, but I took it out. She said, 'You were bad today.' She said I had to stay there till my foster father got home. I was there for a good three hours before dinner. He didn't come home until we just about sat down to eat. She would never bring anything up at the table concerning bad things because it disturbed everybody else's meal. We had pepper and onions that night. I don't like them so I told her, 'I can't eat those things.' She said, 'You are eating them anyhow.' I said, 'No, I am not.' She said, 'Yes you are; don't tell me that you're not or I will shove them down your throat.' I said, 'No, you're not going to feed me either.' So she forced them down me and I heaved up. She made me really sick.

I feel that many many times she tried to kill me. One time it happened in the bathtub. She said, 'I am going to wash your hair.' She dunked me all the way under with my face and nose under too. And she kept me there. I said to her, 'You don't have to be so cruel.' What she told me was, 'Don't talk to me like that – I am your mother.' That time she didn't say foster mother but I knew the difference. She held me under a good one minute at least. I was trying to struggle to get up on top but she just wouldn't let me. I don't think that she really liked me anyways.

Another incident happened when my foster brothers and sisters were standing upstairs in the bedroom. I don't remember their names because there was so many people in my life that names are just names. I remember standing at the top of the stairs and one of her children swore. She blamed me because I was in the crowd. What does she do? She takes me by the back of the collar and throws me down a flight of stairs. I was lying at the bottom of the stairs in a pool of blood and she don't even come running down. She was not even sorry or anything. My foster father came in and says, 'What in the world happened?' There I am laying in a big pool of blood and nobody called the police – nobody did nothing. He was the one who rushed me to the hospital. He didn't take the car; he got the ambulance. I got twenty-six stitches underneath my chin here. I got a good scar still from it. She wasn't sorry for it at all. You know she didn't feel any pain, or no sorrow, no sadness, no nothing. I think she enjoyed doing those kinds of things. There were other incidents. She was just so cruel to me; that is why I disliked her and acted the rottenest and angry and disturbed all the time.

There was another incident that I'll never forget and she won't either. She made me eat something that I couldn't stand again. Then she made me go to bed at 6:00 o'clock because I gave her a hard time. She made me go to bed after my father was through hitting me. My foster father would never say anything to her – let her do anything she wanted and treat me any way. When I gave her a tough time about eating he just came after me with a whip. When he whipped me it was with a horse whip. He didn't use a belt or his hand, he used that whip. I had marks across my back, but since I have gotten bigger they stretched out. He was the one that did the whipping.

That night I remember that I felt the way I felt often – deserted. No one cared and that they were just trying to ruin me. They just didn't care. Sometimes even now I say to people, 'How come you don't care?' I get these little moods. I even did it last night when somebody corrected me on something and I said, 'Well, you don't care anyhow.' We don't change overnight. It is going to take some time to change, to get over what happened to me. Well, anyway, I was there in my bed. It must have been about 2:00 in the morning and I was sick. My foster mother heard me yelling but she wouldn't come to me. She laid right there in that bed and I was heaving up all over the wall and splattering the whole bed. I was just a mess and she says to me, 'You are going to lay in that.' I started to cry. I felt bewildered. I felt nobody cared and everyone hated me. There was no love there, no companion at all, none whatsoever.

I told my foster father in the morning. I was kind of bold. That was the only way I could get something. I couldn't be nice about things, they wouldn't listen. Well, anyways, I had to go to the doctor. I had sores from lying in the barf. My foster mother never told the doctor what she did but I told him. I opened my mouth and says, 'Doctor, I want to tell you how I got this rash.' When I got home I got beat for that and got punished again.

After all this I had had it. I was a little girl. I cried a lot, of course. You are going to cry when you get treated like that. I told them, 'I am going to run away.' They said, 'If you run away, girl, you are going to be sore for more than two days.' I ran away, I did, I took my little feet and went.

I didn't plan to do it that day. I just went to school like I was supposed to. In the morning I did my regular chores. I got the paper, fed the pigs, fed the chickens, pulled some potatoes and stuff out of the garden for dinner and fed the dog. Her kids had hardly anything to do. I was the working girl around there. I finished the chores and ran and got my bus to go to school.

That day was a hard day in school. I had a lot of hard days, but this day I was really bad. I had a hard time because of the way my mother rejected me and the things that were going on – the cruelty, the beating, and stuff. That was uncalled for. I just reacted to it at school. The teachers, they found out. They knew why, I think. The principal on that day said, 'You can't do these bad things. You still have to be corrected. We will have to send a note home.' I told them, 'Don't send any note home any more because I get beat for it.' He said, 'Well, if you are bad and we can't handle you, what are we going to do?' I didn't know what to say to him. I just stood there and I cried.

I knew if a note went home again that was it. I waited till the school bus started to take off and when the counselor came to pick me up I wasn't there. I took off into the woods in back of the school. I didn't know exactly where I was going. What was the sense of going back home? I wasn't getting the love that a little girl needs. They didn't care and if they did they sure weren't showing it. I said to myself, 'There is nothing there for me. If I go maybe I will get another home that will be better.' I was just running – just running because there was no place to go. I thought that I would head for the downtown, but I didn't even know

where that was. I ran and walked and ran and walked and ran
and got tired. I layed down in the woods and went to sleep for a
little while. I was scared because it was the woods and I wasn't
used to sleeping on wet wood. I was afraid of snakes and stuff. I
still fear snakes. I won't go near them or see them or look at them
on TV. I was also afraid that my foster parents would do something if they caught me.

When I got home I was already in tears because I was afraid. I
remember that I was back in that house and I was scared and
crying. My foster mother said, 'What's the matter with you?
Why are you crying?' I said, 'I ran away.' She said, 'Ran away?
From where?' She didn't even know I was gone. See, part of
running away was also thinking that when I came back I might
get some kind of love or attention. Even though she had threatened me about running, I thought she might miss me.

She did talk to me that day. She asked me why I had run away
and I told her that they didn't love me and neither did my foster
father or the kids. I told her about them putting all that junk on
me to do. She gave me time and attention that time. She said,
'What is the problem?' I said, 'I don't like the way you people are
treating me and I would like to go to another place or I would
like you to call my mom and have her come down here and talk
this out.' She said, 'We are not going to have her here. The only
time she can come is when she calls and we give her permission.
She is not going to be allowed to come here.' I said to her, I says,
'You are not fair. My mother is my mother and you are my foster
mother.' I was just seven years old, but I knew. I am no dummy.
I told her that I wanted to talk to my mother and I wanted her to
really know. She said, 'Really know what?' I said, 'Know what is
going on around here.' She said, 'Oh yeah, I am going to tell
your foster father all about this.' I said, 'OK, when he gets home.'
So we got into the living room and she sent all the kids to bed
and we talked about it.

For a little while it was getting better. She wasn't forcing food on
me. When she realized that I didn't like something she wouldn't

make me eat. She would let it go. When it came time to shower, my father said I was old enough to wash my own hair. They started treating me like a person, not an animal. I still had all the chores and they still hit me but I had some privileges like riding the horse and having time off to be by myself. Many times I would do the dishes and help fold laundry and then we would sit and watch soap operas in the afternoon. I would come home from school and I would say that I was sick and she would let me sit there. There were times she was nice, but she made up for them.

Christmas time came around and my father and mother came to visit. I was so happy to see them. They brought me toys. They took me out for a ride. We were in the car. Dad was driving. They were separated but not split up. My dress came open a little bit because I was leaning over to give my mom a kiss and she said to me, 'What is that on your leg?' From being beaten I had a big black-and-blue mark right here on my thigh. I said, 'Nothing.' I tried to sit back and cover it because I didn't want her to see it really. See, I had mixed ideas about what would happen. I was afraid that mom would have an argument and my dad would get into it. And if everyone got going it would make it even worse for me when they left. I was afraid. I wasn't bold enough to show her but when she asked to see it, I did show it. She said, 'What in the hell is that?' I told her it was a black-and-blue mark and then told them how I was whipped with a horsewhip. She told my father to turn the car around to start back.

She went right back to that house. She said to Mrs Mills, 'What do you think this is?' She pulled up my dress. 'Just what do you think this is on my daughter, huh?' Mrs Mills said that I was bad and didn't behave in school and stuff and that I didn't do what I was supposed to. My mother said, 'Well, you don't do that.' My mom was furious, but my dad – you know – was quiet. He just stood right there and let my mom do it all. Mom was bold, she would do anything.

My mommy gave me a kiss and said that she would be back soon and that she would try to get me out of here. I cried, oh did I cry. I hung on to my mom's skirt and I wouldn't let go. I was yelling, 'Don't go. Don't go.' My mother picked me up and held me. They didn't know what was coming off. I couldn't stop screaming. No matter what they did they didn't stop it. My father said to Mrs Mills, 'Would you mind if we took our daughter out for an ice cream?' They knew that I wouldn't calm down unless they took me. I guess I was eight at this time. So they took me for a ride with me sitting between mom and dad. They talked to me – told me not to worry about anything because they were going to find me a new home, told me that she was going to buy me a new dress so that the day when I was going to leave I would be pretty. She told me that my hair would be curled, too. I had real, real long hair. She could do it in ringlets and curls so I really looked nice.

My own parents made me feel better. They told the Mills that they were going to take me to the welfare and have me checked and get me put in another home – a good home. My mother told her, 'I want her cleaned and I mean cleaned. I want her hair washed, I want it set, I want her in the dress I bought her and I want her things packed and ready to go when I get here to pick her up.' My mom also told her that she was going to get her license to have foster children taken away. She told her that she didn't deserve to have welfare children or foster children 'cause she just didn't treat them right.

Capital Children's Home

I don't know how long after that it was but my mom came back and picked me up to go to the welfare department. I recall to this day how she took me from that home, packed everything up in the car, and went. My dad wasn't with her. A woman from the welfare was – my counselor or somebody. I remember, when we got to the welfare, going up the elevator. We went way up and the welfare lady told me to have a seat. She was really nice. I was a little girl and she gave me toys and games and stuff to play with. I was feeling kind of radiant – really peppy and happy. Even now in my life, when I know there is going to be a change-over – a move to a new place, I get really excited and happy. I can't sleep, either. Right now I can't sleep because I know that I am going to move to a new place soon. I was the same way then.

I couldn't stop laughing. Whenever someone would say something I was laughing. I was a little afraid that the new place they would put me in would be worse, but they said it would be better. They said that I would have a happier home, but going through my mind, even at that age, was that them saying it didn't mean anything. Sometimes it happens that way now, too.

So they started calling around to find a place to put me. Where did I end up? Way far away from Penrose. They sent me all the way to Capital Children's Home. It's a place, more or less, for mothers who rejected their children, or people that ought to take care of their children, or couldn't. I went there the same day after my physical. It was a long ride and I was getting tired. We drove down, my mother, the welfare lady, and me. They told me I was going to a home for children and I was going to have counselors that were very nice people. They said I was going to have more freedom and it was going to be nice. The welfare lady said, 'You are going to be able to go to school with children and have a happier time but it is all up to you. You have to make it work too.' She told me my counselor's name, which was Mr Orwell. All the way there I kind of didn't really think. I slept quite a distance. We stopped and got something to eat. I fell asleep on my mom's lap. I was so happy. I kept asking my mom when we were going to be there every few minutes.

There were three cottages – South, East, and West. They were brick and all lined up. There was this office building over to one side and that's where they parked the car. The lady said to me, 'This is the way we have got to go Patricia.' I went in through the door, but I couldn't even open the door I was so excited. Mr Orwell met us. He shook my hand and said, 'This is the young girl that we are going to have, huh?' He was really nice, that really started the whole thing right. Someone had greeted me with a happy smile. From his voice I knew that he was genuinely happy. You know, it wasn't this fake stuff. They sat me down in the office and talked to me and wrote down some things on paper and started getting my papers together. I had a lot of appointments with Mr Orwell. I became a problem child through that home.

I was in school there and it was a good school. I don't remember any teachers. I was there for about two years. It was right in the middle of Capital. I think there were about ten or twelve kids to a cottage. The whole place was like a university campus. In the winter we had an ice-skating rink and they furnished the ice skates for us. They gave us money each month for clothes. They took us shopping in the counselors' cars. The school was on the grounds, but it was little. There was a big gym and three or four classrooms. Some kids went outside to school, but I was one that stayed in 'cause they had to keep observation on me. When you go into a new place like that they like to observe you, to see if you need any help. Maybe you are a little disturbed, you know.

I learned a lot from that school. I learned how to do laundry, and how to clean good, how to set the table, how to make a bed, and how to clean and take care of my clothes – iron and everything. They taught me my adding and subtracting too. We had a guinea pig that the teacher wanted us to get used to. We would read stories and stuff and she would read them to us when we were sitting around in a circle. We would sing and clap our hands.

In our cottage we had a TV with a shelf over it with books on it. Boy, I tell you, it was beautiful. Carpet everywhere except in the dining room and the kitchen. The counselors on duty had their own room. It was a beautiful room. They allowed us to go in there and sit there and talk with them. We had a big huge wood area in the back where we could run around. They would take us hiking through the woods finding leaves and tree bark, maple when it was in season. We would look at all the birds and build caves out of sticks that we could crawl through like tunnels. I was in the Girl Scouts there and the Campfire Girls. We would go out into the woods and light the fires and sit there roasting marshmallows and singing campfire songs. Oh, it was just beautiful.

When I got to Capital, Mr Orwell told me, 'If there is any problem, I want you to tell me right away. I don't want you to hold them in and let them build up.' Pattie never did do what he said. I always let them build up until I exploded.

I will never forget my first experience. The counselor told me to go in and clean out my room. I didn't want to. I wanted to read some books. Well, anyway, she also wanted me to clean the bathtub that everyone in the cottage uses. I told her, 'I'm not cleaning that tub. I didn't use it last.' I got really upset. I put on one of my temper tantrums. I started stomping up and down and banging my head up against the wall. The counselor came in again and said, 'What's the matter, Pattie?' I said, 'I don't want to clean that tub.' I remember that Heather was the one that used it last. She was my girlfriend. I don't remember none of the girls there but her. All this time she has always been in my mind. Well, anyway, the counselor told me, without even checking, 'Heather didn't use it last.' She made me clean it. I don't really remember what I was thinking. I was mad because someone told me to do something. I was in the bathroom steaming angry. I just went out of there and looked and all of a sudden I was throwing things. I went and grabbed the books off the bookcase and threw them across the room. I just ran like a bull and threw everything all over the living room. I turned over the couch. I threw the chairs in the dining room and turned over the tables. Then I went after one of the girls. I didn't hurt her, just went after her, and pulled her hair. I don't know what caused me to do it except

I was plenty angry – that I know. I knew what I was doing. It's not like I was in a trance. I didn't like cleaning that tub. If I did something bad, maybe I would get out of doing stuff. Maybe I did that because I thought that the kids would be nicer to me and I wouldn't get hit. This first tantrum was just a few months after I got there. The first one was like as soon as I realized what everything was all about and I felt more or less free. After that they came frequently.

The counselors treated me nice. There was only one time that I remember that I got slapped. There was only one incident – it wasn't very nice. It was like I was saying that I always had trouble with the other kids. I was pretty good when I was by myself. I am that way now, too. When I was with the other kids, it seemed like I was always getting picked on. They would hit me, throw stones, pull my hair, and try to beat me up. Maybe it was because I pulled myself off into my own little world. I would go on a swing to get away from them. I felt that I was rejecting them. They wanted to play and I wanted to be by myself. I was always a lone person.

Heather and I were buddies. She was my first friend there. I had a couple of friends before, but they weren't close. They would do bad things when I did bad things. That is the kind of friendship we had, but Heather would do good things and bad with me. There were groups of girls that hung out together. They had their little gangs they would go play with, or run into the woods and leave me. Until I left we were really good friends.

We talked together. She would come to my room at night and we would sit and talk. We would play records and talk about something stupid that happened in school – that someone did that was funny. I never told her or anybody about my real feelings. I cried sometimes and she and the counselors would ask me what was wrong, but I never really told them much about mom or dad. I don't know why I didn't talk about them, I didn't even tell it to Mr Orwell much. It was part shame and part embarrassment. When one of the kids would say, 'Where is your mother?'

or, 'Why doesn't she come and visit you?' I would just fold up in my own little world. If someone talked about their mother I would just fold up too. When counselors would mention their mothers or dads I would get right up and leave – go right into my room. To me it was embarrassing. To me it was shame.

I wanted my mom and I've always made it known that I wanted to go back home. I would tell Mr Orwell, 'I want to go back with my mom.' He would say, 'Well, what is it, don't you like us here?' I really couldn't tell him what was really bothering me like I was feeling it. I wasn't able to express myself. When I was a little girl I didn't know how to express the way I really felt because of embarrassment. Anything that really bothered me, I would hide. I didn't want to be looked down at. Some of the kids had moms and dads and some of them didn't. Some people had moms and they could go out and ride around with them. Some had moms that didn't come around.

When I watched television and I saw programs that had families on them – programs like Walt Disney; they didn't have to be families, anything that had something to do with a male or female or mom or dad – I would just get right up and leave or ask the counselors to switch it over to something else. It was tough not telling people about mom and dad – mostly mom – dad didn't mean all that much to me.

We had a lot of disagreements in my cottage. One thing was, they always wanted to listen to records or watch TV, and I wanted to read a book. When I was a little girl I always read out loud. I would sit there in a chair and read. They didn't like that. They wanted to watch their program. I knew that that wasn't really right to do, but I wanted to do it anyhow. What Pattie wants, Pattie wants.

One day they were watching TV and this little girl came up to me and says, 'Can you be quiet? Don't read out loud. I want to watch TV.' They were watching Mickey Mouse on Channel 2. She got really mad with me. I walked up to her and I said, 'Why

don't you shut your mouth? I want to read my book.' I was a
bully with them because I wanted to do what I wanted to do.
That's the reason why I didn't get along too well. So, anyways,
we had a little tussle down on the living-room floor, right in
front of everyone. We were pulling each other's hair and hitting
each other. It was kind of like a serious play fight – we weren't
trying really to hurt. The counselor came and broke it up, and sat
us in the corner, and talked to us. She never hit us. The women
counselors never hit us. Little things like that fight, the women
handled. The men did the hitting. They could send you to them.

All during this time I would have these tantrums and get so
angry. A temper tantrum is when you just jump up and down
and roll around kicking and shouting. It is when you are so
emotional inside. You feel uptight – like you want to kill; that's
it, to kill. I don't know why I got so angry. I have an idea that I
was so bottled up inside – so many things were going through
my mind. I would think, 'Why can't I be home with my mom
and dad? Why do I have to be here with all these children?' I
had temper tantrums at the Mills', too – especially when I got
hit. I would stand there and jump up and down and hit my head
against something, or take my feet and bang it against the door
or the floor. But I don't think that I ever disturbed any of the
furniture or anything the way I did at the Capital Home. I think
that doing that at Capital was because there was too much freedom there. It was freedom that I wanted, but it was too much,
maybe. I think it would have been better if it would have been a
little stricter.

When it came down to it, after I was done doing something
bad, it bothered me. Not until I had done it would it happen.
Then I would sit there and cry. I felt sorry. I got really upset after
I had just done something wicked like destroying furniture or
trying to hurt people. I guess I was very disturbed. I call it disturbed, but it was when I was very upset. A lot of people at
Empire State, the place I went after Capital, told me I was disturbed – that I was disturbed and that I was retarded – so I figure

that all through my life I was disturbed. Looking at the things I done, I must have been disturbed. Disturbed to me is when I am doing bad things like breaking furniture or throwing books. I call that disturbed. Upset and disturbed are the same in my mind. Crazy to me is something else. It is somebody that is really gone. I mean really out. Just deliberately kill somebody just to do it. That is what I call crazy. I guess what I was was emotionally disturbed – yeah. Emotionally disturbed is a time when too many things are bothering me. They just build up till I get so nervous and upset. My mind just goes through all these changes and different things. So many things inside that were bothering me. Thinking about the foster homes and that I had a mom and dad. Why couldn't I be home and be with them? Why couldn't they have straightened out their lives a little bit so that I could have gone home and I wouldn't have had to go through all that I am telling you.

There were lots of fights and I was always getting into trouble. The worst thing that happened was the fire. I think that was the thing that made them say, 'We can't keep her.' The thing happened because my counselor left matches on the table in the living room. They were told that they were not supposed to do that. So, I saw these matches, and I says to Heather, 'Hey, you want to try them?' I didn't really know that much about them. The counselors didn't smoke around us. The agitator, Heather, she says, 'Yeah.' We went in my bedroom and were there trying to get it lit. So it lit and we were so scared by the flame that we just threw it and it went on the bed and then all over. We didn't have time to stop it because the bedding caught on quick. It went to the rug, too. The whole room went up. All my clothes and half of Heather's room too. We didn't do that purposely. I was just exploring. I wanted to see how they worked. Anyways, I said that we better get out of there. Smoke was coming into the hall. Mrs Newman, the counselor, she said to me, 'Pattie, what are you doing?' I started crying and she went to sound the alarm.

There were two wings. The East and the West. I was at the East. We all had to go out the exit on the West because the other was near the fire. We all went over to the gymnasium. Mrs Newman went and told this big husky man counselor what I did. I was sitting there crying and she brings him in.

Want to know what the punishment was? After the fire was out all the kids from my end all came into the living room. I was stood up front and everybody else was on the couch, or chairs, or on the floor. The man counselor came and said, 'Now this is going to show everyone else whoever touches a match what is going to happen to them.' And they sat there wondering what was going to happen – is he going to burn her, or what? He took a chair from the dining room and put me across his knee and spanked me. All the girls looked and I was crying and screaming and he said, 'Now you stand there in that corner and don't you let your nose come up.' I stood there and didn't move either. I was afraid of him. He told Mrs Newman to let me go in a half hour. They got the room back in order. They painted it and got new furniture. I talked to Mr Orwell about it. He told me, 'You girls should know different things, like about matches. How to use a stove and how to cook.'

Mr Orwell and me, we had counseling meetings. He was like my psychiatrist. He had me talk about things, just like the Welfare Department lady did. He could bring things out that other people couldn't. Like why I was fearful – why I was so nervous and jumpy when someone was coming towards me. I couldn't tell other people about some of those things.

Orwell sat me down and gave me tests, too. He gave me blocks and stuff and put me in a room with him. Told me to maneuver the blocks and try to make pictures. He showed me what to do and if I did it he would say how good it was and he would compliment me and stuff.

After a while and after the fire, Mr Orwell called my mom to have a meeting. He told her that I was having temper tantrums and was doing wild things that were turning things upside down there. He said that I was learning OK, but that I was really disturbed. I was turning eleven then and he told me that we had to have a meeting with my mom because I was getting unbearable. They couldn't reach me any more to handle me, I was getting too wild. He told me that maybe they could find another place for me. I told him the reason that I was so wild then. I told because of mom and dad. They didn't come down to see me ever. They came once or twice the whole time I was there; that was from when I was about eight until I was about eleven. I told him, I said, 'Mr Orwell, I know that I've got a mom and dad. Why don't they come down and visit me? Maybe I wouldn't be so bad if I was with them. Why do I have to go through this? Why me? Why can't I go home like a human girl? Why can't I be a normal person with a home, with parents? Why do I have to be in a place like this?' Maybe if I had had more visits – if I knew that they cared. This was during the period that they were trying to get mom together to come to the meeting about me. I was just getting worse and worse – doing badder and badder.

They drew up the meeting and the meeting was about me going to Empire School for the mentally retarded. This was in 1965. After Mr Orwell and my mom got together they sent me out of the room. It was a short meeting. I came back in and he was calling my mother 'Kate.' They thought that the best thing for me was some kind of professional help. They said that I should get it now, early in life, before it would be too late. So they wanted to straighten it out so it wouldn't be so bad in my later years. So that is what they had decided. That I was to go to Empire State School. They said that it would probably be the best right then, because it was the only place they could think of, I guess. Really, what other alternatives did they give my mom?

Admission to the State School

They said that Empire would be the only school that would help me. They also thought I needed learning in how to cook. I didn't

know what Empire was. The first time I walked into the building
to be admitted that was the first time I heard retardation. I didn't
really know what I was in for. I just accepted going.

I can't recall just how many weeks or how many months it
was after Mr Orwell's and mom's meeting that I went. All's I
remember is having all my things packed and being ready. He
went with me to Empire. I think he drove me, or my mom drove
her car. It is just not all that clear in my mind. I cried, because I
didn't know what was going on.

All's that I know is we got there and drove into this huge
place. There were these big brick buildings – and I mean big. It
looked weird. I mean it looked just like a prison – all these brick
buildings standing there in the middle of the wilderness. It was
right in the middle of the country and the first thing that came to
mind was the wilderness. The buildings were tall and dreary
looking – ugly looking. The windows didn't have any shades on
them and they had bars on them. We went around the back of
the buildings and then in front of old X Building, C Building, G
Building. Right past the boiler house or the power house as
they called it. We stopped at the administration building which
was called B Building at that time. This was in the fall of '65 I
think.

The people were around gawking. I thought I was coming into
some place where they were all out to vulture me – eat me up,
devour me, or something, because of the way the people were
gawking. They drove the car up and people stared out of the
windows. Here I am a stranger to the place. It was bad enough
just looking at the buildings, but seeing the people made it worse
yet. They were handicapped. Some of them were deformed. A lot
of them looked like me, but a lot of them weren't normal.

Some had little legs or deformed feet or something. Out by the
baby building they had babies out in strollers. Their legs were up
over by their necks. There were quite a few people on the
grounds all over the place just standing and looking. I saw these
people looking at me. I was scared. I didn't want to go in, but my
mom said, 'It's all right. It's all right.'

I walked into the administration building and the first thing somebody said was, 'Oh, we have a new girl here.' That is what they called me for a whole week, 'New Girl.' I was thinking to myself, 'What is this place? What are they going to do to me?' More or less I was thinking, 'Why am I here?' The first thing I thought about the place was that it would be the kind of place that you wouldn't have any freedom at – that you would be locked in for a good long time. I saw some people that looked like me, but I remember saying to myself, 'What am I doing here? I don't deserve to be here. I don't have any problems.' I talked to someone and asked her why I was there and she told me that I was there because they felt I needed to be.

I was afraid, walking into that administration building. I walked in with Mr Orwell and my mom. They saw my reaction to the place because I was crying. They said, 'She'll be OK.' I said to them, 'Don't leave. Please, I want you to stay around for a little while.' An attendant and a Dr Shoemaker – she was a lady – she told me, 'You are going to like it here.' I said, 'Yeah?' The attendant said, 'Are you going to eat? It is good food. You really need to eat after driving all that way.' I sat down, but I couldn't eat. The stuff looked like ground puke, really. It was terrible – ground food. Ground meat, ground vegetables, and milk. I said, 'I don't want this.' Mr Orwell said, 'Don't make her eat it.' So we had lunch in this little room in the administration building. There were other people, too, who must have been being admitted or discharged or something.

After lunch they told me that I could visit with mom and Mr Orwell until things got ready for my physical and stuff. They told me that the doctor would check me and talk with me and then I would get a shower and that they would give me clothes. They were going to take my clothes that I brought. I couldn't wear them. I thought about what kind of clothes they were going to give me – were they going to be ugly, dirty, and dreary look-ing? When I did see them I said, 'I'm not wearing them.' My mom told me that wearing the clothes was just part of getting used to the place. She asked them if I had to wear them and they **113** said nobody was allowed to wear their own clothes. There were these ugly grey slacks that they gave me, and an ugly old shirt. My mom said, 'Well, I have to go now. I have really got to get back. I don't want to leave, but I have to go and so does Mr Orwell.' They left together.

I cried – oh, I screamed and went through one of my fits. The doctor came and said that I would be all right. They left me in this room waiting to be examined. I was still screaming, 'I want to go home. I don't want to stay here.'

The first thing that they did was stick a thermometer in my cula. I hated that because I was used to having it done by my mouth. Now this physical happened – now I remember – over in the admissions building. They took me over there after lunch. Having that thermometer was a scary thing. It was a frightening feeling. I thought they were trying to hurt me. They checked my heart and things, and looked all over me for scars. They put them down if you had any, so if anything happens there they won't be blamed for it.

All the people were in uniforms, white uniforms, all white. They had caps on if they were senior attendants and they had two black stripes across the cap. If they were juniors they had just one stripe. They took me out of the examination room and took me and put me on a table like a little baby and showered me. I was ten years old and they showered me. The attendants were the ones who did that. They had this spray hose that they used. It was like a big bathtub, but it didn't have much water in it, or high sides, but it was off the floor. The attendants could stand there and you would be right next to them. They strapped me into the tub. It was like a strap around my belly. They put that on you so you wouldn't fall out if they left. I didn't like that bath. I wanted to bathe myself. I felt that they were just treating me like a baby, and they were. They hurt me when they washed me because they used a scrub brush, a wash cloth, and brown soap. The brown soap is harsh.

There were two of them that washed me. They took my clothes completely off. I was embarrassed being naked in front of them, in front of everybody, because I am used to being by myself. After they finished the bath, then I had to do a urine test. I said, 'Where's the bathroom?' and it was right in the same room as that bathtub. The toilets were all open. They didn't have any doors on them. I asked them where the doors were. I knew that much, that there are supposed to be doors on toilets. They told me that they didn't have any there because they had to watch the people so they didn't do anything they weren't supposed to do. I told them that I wouldn't do anything, but they said that they had to do it for everybody.

There were other kids on the ward where this all was happening. They didn't shut the door in the bathroom either. There were people sitting out there in the day room watching and there were people running in and out. So I sat down and gave a specimen. It was really disgusting. I didn't feel good at all. In fact I was sick for a couple of days because I was so upset. None of the other wards had toilets with doors, either. Or seats, either. They didn't want people to throw things down the toilet – that was it. I also had to give a couple of stool specimens before I left that building. After they gave me the shower, and I gave them the urine, I was admitted and that was it.

I stayed on the ward where I was showered for six weeks. It was the admission ward. Right after the shower they didn't let me wear the clothes they gave me. They put me in this long gown. It was plain white and it tied in the back. No slippers, or socks, or anything. Then they put me in a crib kind of a bed that had sides on it. It was all white and it was on wheels. There were bars on the sides. They also put me in diapers for a couple of days. I don't know why. I guess that is one of the things they do. I didn't try to tell them I didn't need them. I just let them do it because I knew they weren't going to listen to me anyways. I felt that that was just part of being admitted. They came around at night and they changed me. That was embarrassing. I can't stand

it. They also gave me a bottle with ground food in it. I had to
suck out of that for a few days. They wouldn't let me eat off a
plate. When my mom was there, you better believe they let me
eat off a plate with a spoon. Maybe they were doing all this
because I cried a lot.

Those first few days I don't think I was thinking anything
much. I felt terrible. I was so exhausted and tired from all that
handling and pushing and going through the excitement of getting there. After the first night – I cried most of the night – I
woke up and it was time to eat. Do you know what they did?
They put me in a high chair and they tied a bib around me. They
made me feel just like a baby. I really did. A bib, diapers, and a
bottle at night, and I was ten years old. That's pretty bad. What I
did was I messed in my food. I played with it and took the food
out and played in it. I threw it. They came up to me and said,
'Did you eat your food like a good girl today?' I didn't say anything. I just started to cry because I was afraid of them from all
the things they did before. They were rough with me. They
snapped at you and pushed you. When they put me in the high
chair it was like an instinct to act like a baby.

With all those people dressed in white uniforms, and the beds
white, and the towels white, I felt like I was in a hospital. It
wasn't anything like a school. I started thinking that something
happened to me or something. I thought that maybe I had gotten
sick and I had to be in the hospital for that. I thought that maybe
I needed help to get better. I remembered way back when my dad
threw me across the room. Mom thought that I could have been
damaged from that, but there were no signs of it. She always said
that that was probably why I had all my temper tantrums. I
remember she said that when we were having our meeting in
Capital. My mom came to visit a few times at Empire and she
said the same thing. I couldn't see that. I think me going to
Empire was just plain ignorance and laziness and stupidity from
my family. They didn't want to help me. Throw me in a stupid
school like that.

They kept you on admissions for six weeks so they could observe you. They tested you, and Dr Shoemaker put me on medication. They said I was a very nervous child. The first day, and they put me on Mellaril.[1] They kept upping how much they gave me until I was up to 150 and then they switched me to Thorazine.[2] But I got worse and worse. They just treated you awful. They would come by and wipe your face off with a washcloth while they held down your hands. After breakfast they would take you out of the high chair and put you back in bed for a nap. They would leave you there and never come to check on you or anything. It was like that six weeks. It was mostly from the high chair to the crib and from the crib to the high chair.

As you can guess I wasn't very happy. They did bring a teacher around once a day and they took us to the movies. They treated you very different off the ward. It was like they didn't want the other people to know how nasty they were. But once we got back it was the same stuff. After the first week, they didn't bathe me the way they did first. They would line us up, and take us in one by one under a big shower, and scrub us. I would never prescribe that for anybody. I wish they would have knocked that school down.

The admission ward was locked, and so were most of the wards in the whole school. The ones in X, E, O, R, and Q buildings was. They were all locked so you couldn't go out the door if you wanted to. There were no windows to break either. There was a small window, but they were unbreakable. There was no toys to play with. They had toys, but they kept them in the other room, and they wouldn't let us in there to play with them. The day room was just a big empty place with chairs in it. The floor was dark brown. There were people of all ages on the ward too. Elderly and young kids like me. The cribs were all lined up like in a dormitory room. They even put some of the elderly people

1 Mellaril (generic name: thioridazine hydrochloride) is one of a class of tranquilizing drugs known as phenothiazines.
2 Thorazine (generic name: chlorpromazine hydrochloride), like Mellaril, is a tranquilizing drug belonging to the phenothiazine class.

in the high chairs, and they tied them in there so they couldn't **117**
wiggle out. The food was terrible too.

On admissions we went to bed at 6:00 or 7:00. If you didn't
want to go to bed they made you go. The attendants would tie
you down. I got tied down a couple of times. I wouldn't stay in
my bed. They used ripped-up sheets to do it.

I think it was in admissions when they gave me an IQ test. I got
a few tests there, and they tested me at Capital too. I remember
taking one test. It was like school work – adding and subtracting.
They tested me to see where they would put me I guess. I found
out that my IQ was 72. I remember somebody I never saw before
sat me down and gave me a pencil and told me that I should try
to do the best I could. I did my best, but then they wouldn't tell
me what my score was. I found out when I got older that it was
72. It's a lot higher than that now. When they gave me tests I
didn't ask too many questions because some things that they
said didn't even make any sense to me.

A lot of people came in and out of that ward. They would
come in and say, 'Hi – what's your name?' I would say Pattie.
They would ask me how old I was and I would say eleven. They
would ask me if I like it there and I would say, 'No.' They would
say, 'You will like it once you get used to it.' I think a doctor
came in to talk to me once. They took me to a private room so we
were alone. I don't remember what they did or what they said,
but I heard that they were going to transfer me over to O Building to be with girls my own age. They told me that I would be
able to walk downstairs to eat in the cafeteria. I was a little
frightened, but I was looking forward to it. They told me that I
would be on a big ward. I would have attendants there, maybe
three or four, and eighty-two people.

O Building

After they looked me over for six weeks and gave me tests and
everything, they sent me over to O Building. I stayed there,

except when I was punished, until I went to Central City. Like I said there were over eighty people on my ward. The kids were from about eight to seventeen years old but, come to think about it, Meg Brock was only five, so some of them were younger. We were in this big three-floor building with two wards on each floor. The ward next to us was O–15. That was mostly retarded children. You know, very retarded chlidren. They would rock back and forth and play with a piece of string with their fingers. Just look at it and wiggle it around like this. Some wet their pants right there, and they would have to shower them.

Downstairs, there was O–14, and that was for older girls from let's say eighteen to forty or so. They were good. A lot of them were smart. Next to that was O–17, and that was for parole people. That's for girls that was going out into the community. O–18 was upstairs, and that was for the older women – the grannies. There was a basement in O which was our cafeteria-style dining room. No people lived down there. There were over eighty people on each ward, and six wards. That's a lot of people. They had great big dormitories that lined up four or five rows of beds. The dormitories were huge. Eighty-two people slept in one room on my ward.

The ward they put me on wasn't the type for residents that looked at their fingers all day. They were school-age children that could learn. They had minor problems like home problems – they didn't have any place to go. Some kids were on medication because they were highly disturbed and they would go around acting up, by throwing things and stuff.

The day room was this one huge room that we spent the day in. We had chairs in the day room. They used to more or less split us into three groups, and they had three different sets of chairs. There were the five-to-ten year olds, the ten-to-fifteen year olds, and then those over fifteen. They arranged the chairs so that the groups would kind of be by themselves. Everybody kind of sat in their own square. The attendants had their place way in the back near Mrs Black's desk. She was the charge. They

used her desk to keep the records. Whenever we did something   **119**
wrong they would put it in the record. If we were acting up at
night or something, they would put us to bed, or give us a cold
shower, and then write us up. Even if we got upset or angry they
would write it up on a piece of paper. The TV sat up high on a
shelf at one end right near the desk. One attendant always sat
there and watched us. Sometimes she would walk around to find
out where the voices were coming from.

When I first went to O Building, I was thinking about what
might be wrong with the girls. I visited other wards and knew
that there was something either mentally or physically wrong
with most. Gradually, I didn't pay it much mind. When I was
that age I really didn't put much thought into things like that.
We were all in the same boat, more or less. We would talk about
school and how we didn't like some of the attendants. Sometimes at night we would start planning on how to act up when
an attendant came on that we didn't like. We didn't talk much
about the other kids on the other wards, as I remember.

All the kids on my ward weren't the same. Some of them
were slower than others. Some played by themselves most of
the time. Some read books or just walked around. Some just sat
in the middle of the day room and watched TV all day long. We
didn't make fun of people on the ward. We weren't like that at
all. Nobody on the ward made fun of anybody. I mean when
someone got you angry or something you would say, 'Oh, you
dummy,' or, 'Stupid,' or something, but nothing out of place.

Going to my ward the first day was strange. We walked up to it.
One of the nurses from where I was in the admitting building
brought me. They introduced me to my attendants and then they
took my clothes and put them in the clothes room. I said, 'What
are you doing with my clothes?' They said, 'We are taking them
to the clothes room where everybody else's are.' I asked them
what a clothes room was and they showed me. You know, they
took me all around the ward. They showed me the dormitory

and everything. They were really nice to me – boy, they were as nice as pie. Nobody was mean. They didn't even look at me cross-eyed, but then about a week passed, and before I knew it I was getting hit with sticks and put into cold showers.

It always takes me time to get used to a new place. I got used to the way the others were acting on O and thought to myself, 'Well, I'm going to be a part of this game. I'm going to start acting like them.' So I did. I did some bad things that some of the kids did.

The first time I got in trouble was about a week after I got there. We always had to line up to go to the bathroom. We lined up for everything – to eat, to go to school, to the movies, to go here and there. Two by two we lined up. I was in line, a big long line, to go to the bathroom. Now nobody wants to stand in a long line like that to go. So I was upset and I said, 'I don't want to stand here in this line.' The attendant said, 'You get back in line where you were.' I said, 'No, I got to go. Right now.' Well, anyway, I went in my pants. In the other building that I came from you didn't have to wait. I was used to that. One of the kids said, 'Somebody pissed in their pants back here.' Then everybody just cracked up.

So I got hit on the knuckles. They would take a stick and hit you right across the knuckles. They called it a paper stick. It was that little stick that the toilet paper went on. They would hit you if you got out of line. That time, those that laughed got punished too. They didn't get to go to the movies like we usually went on Friday night. You couldn't talk in line either. You had to be very quiet and stand there like at attention.

It wasn't fair for them to be punished for laughing, but I was glad that I didn't have to stay back on the ward by myself. When you were punished you had to get on your hands and knees and scrub and wax the dormitory floor – that was buffing it, too, and not with a machine but with a rag. I'll tell you, not too many people wanted to be acting up on Fridays.

Not all eighty-two people lined up to use the toilet. They took us in groups according to our ages. You could use the toilet other times, too, if they let you. You had to ask them, but they wouldn't always let you. They didn't trust us in there alone. Sometimes they locked it and you almost had to go in your pants. Everybody had to line up three times a day – morning, afternoon, and before supper – that is, if you had to go or not. Shower time was the same thing. They took you by rows, but we didn't shower every day. They would say, 'OK, big girls come now.' They almost never called us by name. Once in a while you would hear, 'Pattie, come on,' or, 'Meg, come on,' but mostly it was 'OK, come on, girls.' That's the way the attendants were. When they talked to us it was mostly orders. 'Come on, let's go,' 'Hurry up,' 'Get this line straight.' Do this and do that. That's why I won't go in the service. They want me to go. I can't do it – no way.

The bathrooms were small. We only had three toilets and they were close together. They had one shower. They started using the shower in the bathroom downstairs, which had five showers in it. There you were able to sit on benches or stand up to wait your number. There we had three in the shower at one time.

Thinking about it now, after you waited in line to use the toilet, you sat down and they rushed you. They would say, 'Come on now. Somebody else has got to go.' You couldn't really do anything if you had to. There wasn't always toilet paper in there either. Sometimes we had to go without it. You had to ask for toilet paper. Sometimes they wouldn't let us have it, because some girls would bundle it up and throw it. They would tell you that you couldn't have it because people were wasting it. They would give you a few pieces that they would tear off the roll and that would be it.

The reason that the attendants punished us was because they didn't want to work hard. They were always having people polishing the floor. We did the whole big day room. We have about five or six people doing it. They would pick us out. If we were talking when we weren't supposed to, or if we didn't raise our hand, they would make us polish. Every time we opened our mouths they would have us down there cleaning and polishing.

If they said all day, you did it all day. You could stop and eat. They made sure you did that.

We had lockers to keep our stuff in, but we weren't allowed to have the keys. They had to open it. We would have to get something. You kept personal things like rings, necklaces, books, your diary, dress gloves. We wore state clothes, but on special occasions – like, if they knew my parents were coming – they would put you in your own clothes.

When I was on Thorazine I was getting them and throwing them down the toilet. They were saying that the pills weren't doing anything. Of course they weren't. They found out what I was doing. I didn't want to take them. I didn't like them. They just made me sleepy and tired. I couldn't study in school. I couldn't go to school and work or anything like that. I would just fall asleep. They told the doctor about me throwing them away so she put me on liquid medication and I had to stand in front of the attendant until it was all down. Then that stuff began to burn my tongue so they put me back on the pills.

There were a lot of people on tranquilizers – maybe 50 percent of the patients. You could tell who was on it because they would be falling asleep. A lot of them were quiet. They couldn't do some of the things they were doing before.

I started blooming at eleven. I remember that because they told me that they didn't wear brassieres. 'Here, we wear undershirts.' I told them that I had to wear something. They made this cotton brassiere which made me flatter than a pancake. It had two buttons in the back.

When there was no school we just sat in the day room and watched TV. Sometimes there was a special hour for us to go out and play on the playground, but most of the winter we stayed in all the time. I guess it was hard getting us all to dress up, and it was very cold most of the time. The place was very flat, so there was no place to go sliding.

Every day at 6:00 in the morning we had to get up. You see, they had one night watch that would go around at night and check on us – make sure that everybody was sleeping and in their own beds. Sometimes people would crawl under their beds and slept. I think they felt more secure down there. They didn't want people sleeping on the floor. That's why she did the checking. In the morning at 6:00 she came around and turned on all the lights. It was so bright in there that when you opened up your eyes you had to squint. She would just scream, 'Everybody up. Let's go,' real loud. Just wake everybody right up. If someone didn't get up she would go bang you with the window pole. You know, one of those poles that got a little hook on it to open the big windows. They would start screeching at her, 'Don't hit me,' and she would go bang. The pole was real long and she used it to reach people so she didn't have to walk around. I got hit with it once. She didn't use the end with the hook on it. She would hit with the other end – get you on the leg, or something. See, some girls would like to crawl right back in and go back to sleep, but she would go bang.

We had to strip our beds – that means the sheets, pillows, and blankets, and fold them in a neat pile at the foot of the bed. After folding everything up you would have to stand by your bed or sit on it and wait for your group to be called to wait in line for the bathroom. This is all before 7:00 o'clock when we had breakfast. Before breakfast you would get dressed. The clothes were right at the foot of our beds. When you went to bed at night, you folded what you had on up and put them underneath the mattress. We got clean clothes three times a week when we got our shower. When everybody was ready we would all sit in the day room and wait for the bell. The bell would be rung from the cafeteria telling us that it was our turn to go downstairs. While we were waiting, two girls would be called by the night watch to go and make sure everything was straightened out – that the beds were lined up just right – we had like invisible lines that we had to put those beds on. We didn't make the beds when we woke up because that was for the day shift to make us do. It was hard just getting the kids up and getting them moving before breakfast.

While we were waiting, the day shift would come on. They would say, 'Good morning, girls.' We would say, 'Good morning,' and that would be it. See there were three shifts that kept coming and going. The day shift was on at 7:00. There were three or four on the day shift. Sometimes they were sick and we only had two. Two could manage though, I'll tell you. They knew how to manage. They would say, 'OK, girls. It is 7:00 –' there was a big clock up there on the wall where you could see it '– let's go. Everybody stand up.' We would stand up and they would have us stretch and then line up. Everybody had to get in the line according to how big you were. Then they would tell us to be quiet and we would walk down to the dining room. Anyone caught talking would be punished. They would have you scrub the stairs or something.

When we got downstairs we would stand and wait there to get our trays. The trays had sections for your food and you ate right off the tray. You would then walk through the line where the kitchen people were handing out the food. If you liked it or not, you had to get everything put on your tray. If you were caught sneaking without anything that was on the menu you were in trouble. At the end of the line, the senior attendant would put your coffee, tea, or milk on the tray. Milk was only for the kids. Tea and coffee for the older ones. Then we would go to our own tables. We knew exactly where we were to sit – the table and the chair. We could go from one table or chair to another. The attendants would go around giving our bread and buttering it for the kids that couldn't. Some kids wouldn't eat by themselves. They were the ones that were closer up to the front. People would feed them.

If you didn't like the food somebody would feed you, too. Sometimes they were mean. One little girl got sick off of something and she didn't want to eat it. They told her that she had to eat to get strong and they held her hands behind her back and said, 'You gotta eat it. It is good for you. You want to get strong. You are only a pipsqueak.' She spit it back up and they fed it

right back to her again. They were going to make her no matter **125**
what. They threatened me that they were going to feed me, but
they never did. They did punish me for not eating, though. The
food was good. Some of it, not all of it. Some of it looked like it
was thrown back up or something.

After everything was over, they had some big girls come by
with a cart and pick up all the trays and stack them up and
scrape them off. Another girl would come behind her with a big
bowl and a sponge and wipe off all the tables. Then everybody
sat back and we would say grace. Everybody said grace. We had
one grace that we all said every meal. I forgot it now, but it went
something like, 'Bless this food.' It has been so long that it is hard
to remember. Nobody could get up, unless you were a helper,
until after grace. Then everybody just fell out in a line from the
table. You'd go back upstairs without talking. Then we would
line up outside the bathroom again and brush our teeth.

After that the little kids didn't have to do anything. They just
had to get their coats and hats on and sit in their chairs. The girls
from ten and up had to do all the beds. We would take disinfec-
tant and wipe them all down from the white tops to the springs.
Then we would make the beds, two girls working on a bed. The
beds had to be just right. The corner had to be right and the
spread too. There was a white bedspread on every bed. Then we
had to dust. They would give a girl an aisle to do.

Then you went to get your coat to go to school. Some girls
didn't have school. They hung around the day room, or cleaned
it. Almost everybody on my ward went to school but there were
many times that we didn't have school because the teacher was
sick or something. They didn't have substitute teachers if a
teacher was sick. I was on medication a lot, so when I went to
school I didn't do much because I slept a lot. They would line us
all up and march us over to school two by two. It was a good ten
minutes walk. After they dropped us off, the attendants took off.
The school was right on the grounds. They had a big gymnasium, cooking class, home economics. That is where I learned

how to cook, but I didn't learn much else. At lunch time they would line you up again and you would walk back to the ward. Use the bathroom again, and line you up to go downstairs. Then we would line up and go back to school.

Wherever we walked any place, one attendant would be at the head of the line, one in the middle, and one at the end. They did that to make sure that everybody was in line and nobody took off. Lots of times the girls would run away. We would stay at school until three and then march back to the building again. For the rest of the day we usually hung around the day room – read books, or watched TV. We had to line up and go into the dormitory and take the spreads and fold them back to get ready for the night. We had to pull the blankets down on the bed in accordion style so we would just have to pull them up when we got to bed. Then we had to be lined up again for supper and we went through that whole thing again. Then the third shift would be on, and they would let us play games if we had been good. The shifts went from 7:00 to 3:00, 3:00 to 11:00, and 11:00 to 7:00. We went to sleep at 9:00. That was the curfew. Everybody except the little kids went to bed then. I think they went at 7:30 or 8:00.

It was on Monday, Wednesday nights, and Saturday morning that we went down and had showers. Every month we had our hair cut. They would have a barber that worked at the place come onto the ward. They would just snip it off. Everybody's hair was just to the end of the ear lobe. The reason was because of the lice. I had beautiful long hair right down to the middle of my waist when I first went there, but they cut it off. I could have killed them. I liked my hair, you know. Some girls had it cut up to about over their ears. I don't know why, but probably it was because they had lice. There was one time I remember when somebody went home on a vacation and brought lice or something back and we all had to have our hair done with Kwell. We had to sit in the chair and let the attendants rub this gooky white stuff all through it. Then they would comb it through with a fine comb to see if we had any lice or anything.

When anybody got real sick, they would rush them right off to the hospital and you never knew what was wrong with them or what happened to them. If you got sick with something it was just passed right around to everyone. There were thousands of people there, so it went through just like fire in the field.

When I think back, the thing that stands out in my mind was the ward and the way it was. You always were in a routine. Going here – lining up and lining up and lining up. At that time I didn't think about it much, but now it seems like it was a prison. Line up, demand, demand, demand. Very seldom did anyone have a kind word to say to us. If you swore or something, you got Epsom salts put in your mouth. *They* could swear at *you*, though. I remember that stuff burnt your tongue. Marilyn Johnson she used to get it, too, She was something. Later on she came to Cornerstone State School and we were on the same ward there. She would be swearing – it was our favorite thing at Empire. She would have the salt put in her mouth. If you wouldn't stop they would send you to the doctor.

The doctor would come on the ward every morning and she would sit behind this desk and look over the records. If an attendant wrote you up for being bad you would have to see the doctor. I couldn't sleep the whole night if the attendants told me, 'I wrote you up and you're going to have to see the doctor tomorrow.' The attendants would write anything in the book they wanted to. If they really wanted to make it tough for you, they would – there was many times that they did. The doctor would just come – for no specific purpose, but to see those that they told to stay back from school. She would come about 9:00, when the kids were gone. If you were sick or written up, the senior attendant would come on and say, 'Stay after breakfast is over. Pattie, stay back from school.' If she said that, you knew right away that it wasn't anything good that would happen.

You would sit in a row of chairs facing the doctor when she came in. You had to stand when she came through the door. Had to stand up to show respect. It was stupid really. We were afraid of her, but we didn't respect her. She would say good morning. I didn't say good morning back, because I knew when I got to her it wouldn't be a good morning. I would just stand there and think, 'Oh, boy, I wonder what's going to happen to me today. Am I going to be sent to Q Building?'

If you were bad, she would read what you had done out of the book first, and then she would say, 'OK, Patricia – up here.' You would come up there and she would tell you to kneel down in front of her. Anybody that was there because they were bad had to kneel. She would tell you that the reason she wanted you to kneel was so that she could see your face. She was a small woman and she would look right down on you. I hated that. I hated the way she would say, 'Now what is the big idea of you acting up like this? Why do you swear all the time?' She would go on, and said, 'Why do you do this and that. I would say, 'Well, sometimes there are people bothering me.' She says, 'Don't tell me that. You just do it.' I told her that wasn't so, and she would tell me not to talk back to her. She would say, 'I don't want to hear that. Shut up.' She wanted to know and when I would tell her she would tell me to shut up. She would get really upset. Then she would say, 'OK. I am going to have to send you to G Building for a couple of days. I really want you to work there. I am going to come down there to see that you are working hard.' Which was a lie 'cause she wouldn't come onto that ward. She told me that if I did anything bad down there they would send me to Q Building. I never went to Q Building, but people that went there told me it was worse than G–2. The first time that I knew I was going to G, I cried. The doctor told me that she didn't want to hear that, and that I should go back to where I was standing. After the doctor left, I begged the attendant not to send me, but she says, 'See Pat, I told you. You should be nicer.'

She would talk real nice to me and I would start crying all the more and say, 'I don't want to go. I don't want to go.' I told them that they could punish me here, but they said doctor's orders. Of all the punishments they could dish out, G was bad, but Q Build-

ing was the worst. Boy, people that went there would cry their **129**
heads off, because you had to do these things there.

Like I said, I never went to Q, but some of the girls told me
about it. That was where the wheelchair patients were. They
were emotionally disturbed – really, really disturbed all the time.
I mean they would hurt people and do things to hurt themselves.
They would have to clean them just like you had to do at G, but it
was worse. They had to clean the sanitaries from the patients –
you know, those things that you wear when you have your
period. You had to clean them. I don't want to talk about it
because it was so gross. You had to scrub them and they used
them over again. Every time you were sent there you had to do
that. I tell you, it choked you up. You would have to scrub them
with brown soap and hang them up to dry.

We didn't have to do that on G – Thank God! It was bad
enough cleaning someone's rear end when they go to the bathroom but sanitaries – ugh! They had other punishments in Q
building. If you gave the attendant a real hard time, like you ran
around and started screaming and disturbing other people, then
they wrote you up. If you only did little stuff, like making noise
in the circle, they would put you in the broom closet. It was high
and it had a lock on it. They would just shove you in there and
lock it. Then they would take the key and they would say, 'Now,
when you get over your nastiness or your meanness you can
come out.'

They would give you cold showers sometimes, too. Mrs Green, I
remember her so well, she would like giving people cold showers
when they were bad. She said that it calmed them down. It made
me all the worse. I didn't like that. They would just throw you
right in there under that cold water and then bring you right
out. She pulled me by my hair. I didn't have much hair on my
head at the time either. After, I got dried and put on dry clothes.
One time I threw a chair because I didn't want to do what she
told me. She said, 'Get the chair.' I said, 'Get it yourself, you
damn fool.' I got a cold shower for that. There is no way you can

refuse a cold shower. They were strong enough to get you in there no matter how hard you would fight. After you had a cold shower you would scream at them, because you didn't want to go back in there.

There was this one time, it was Halloween night. They shut out the lights because they said that we were going to celebrate Halloween. I was sitting in the middle and some of the kids were scared. They didn't like being in the dark. We all started screaming. They told us not to talk or anything because they were going to tell a story. You know if you are going to hear one of those stories, you are going to scream – if it is a spooky one. They screamed. We all had to line up and we all got whipped. That was just because we screamed. One person started it and everybody else did it.

I remember that clearer now. I remember that time when they whipped us that they picked out two big girls from the last row. Mrs Kowalski was on that night – she was short and she couldn't handle us kids by herself. So she used the bigger girls to help her. She put them side by side on each side of the big long clothes table. She took a rubber – you know, the kind you wear in the rain. Two of them held us and the other hit us on the rear end with it.

Everybody in the whole room got hit for it. I didn't think that was right, but what could I say? I went out laughing because it really didn't hurt that much. She said, 'You stand on the side. You are coming back for another dose.' Me and this other girl was all that was left. She laughed too. The second time we didn't. We cried and screeched. Boy, I'll tell you. I don't think I sat down for a while. After they were finished hitting us they made us stand at attention with our hands stretched out until our arms got so sore we couldn't do it any more. But they kept saying to keep them out there. It wasn't that often that everybody got punished like that.

I remember so well Mrs – Oh, what was her name? I can't remember her name but she had this favorite punishment of putting people on the log. We had a chimney, but we never used it – it was just there. They had logs in it and she would say, 'OK, Pattie. I saw you talking. Go get one of those logs.' I would, and then she would send me by the fireplace, in front of everyone, and kneel on that log with my bare knees. That hurt. You would have to stay there at least an hour. Then she would say, 'Well, did you learn anything?' I would say, 'Yeah.' She would say, 'No, I don't think that you did. Kneel back down.' Not everyone punished on the log. Only one attendant did that. The others – it was like each person had their own way of punishing. The night shift, if you were bad with them, they would make you scrub all the stairs right down to the basement. I tell you it was no fun. By the time you got to pass the door to your own ward you were exhausted and your knees were hurting. If you told them to go to hell or something like that they would slap you in the mouth. It would depend on who the attendant was – if you got slapped or not.

I was put in straitjackets plenty of times. When you were put in one, the doctor would have to order it. The attendants had to call the doctor and say, 'Pattie is acting up today. Maybe if we restrained her she would be better.' They always had to call to ask permission. The doctor would say, without even talking to me, 'OK. Put her in it for an hour or so and she will calm down. Put her in a corner away from everybody.'

The first time I went in I didn't want to go, and I fought. I threw a chair and I think I hit one of the residents. I didn't hurt her, but I did hit her. I was mad and I just heaved the thing. I don't remember this clearly anyways. It was hard to live with all those people. There was no privacy. Everybody had to undress in the dormitory and there was no privacy. You would get upset. I told them that I wanted my mom. I wanted to go home. I wanted to leave there. I didn't want to stay. Well, anyways, I was put in the straitjacket and, the first time, it took four people to get me in. When I heard that the straitjacket was coming, I almost went berserk – that's why they had such a hard time. I just dumped myself on the floor and screamed and kicked. They pushed my arms in there and put them way up here in the back and it hurts. They told me that if I didn't calm down they would call the doctor to give me a hypo – it's a needle with medicine in it. I quieted down when they said that. They put me in the corner and wouldn't let me go down to eat. When you're in a straitjacket you are all bundled up and tagged – no freedom. You are angry. I felt like nobody cared. That was their easy way of getting out of things. Instead of trying to sit down and working it out, they put you in there. I was in a straitjacket – let me see – twice in G Building and more than that in O.

I haven't told you about G yet. G Building was for real severely retarded older women. They messed their pants and wet themselves. They would have strings around their fingers and they would whirl the string and look at it. Some of them had bald heads. They would send us over there when we were punished. That was really a sad case when I went over there. They would throw up after they ate and we had to clean it. That was our punishment – cleaning those people in the shower wasn't any fun, either, because they would hit you and pull your hair and stuff.

One time they put me in a straitjacket in G was this one time they got us up at 4:00 in the morning to trip those patients. Tripping them is taking them to the bathroom, and making sure that they went. I was really upset about them waking me up. I was angry, so I took one of the patients and pushed her head in the toilet. The attendant found out and I got put in it that morning. They did let me go back to bed, but on it went in the morning. They tied me to a chair. When they let me out I had to scrub all the toilets.

One time I pushed a polisher in front of one of the attendants and I was sent to G–6 for a month. I don't know how many times I was sent there. It was quite frequently. The first time I was there I didn't know too much about it. The other girls didn't tell **133**

me much. They wanted me to find out for myself, I guess. Once the doctor said that I was going, they didn't waste any time. They sent your papers along with you. The attendant took me down. They said, 'This is Pattie. This is the one that is being punished. Don't give her an easy time. Make her work.' After the first time I was sent there, I started watching other people being punished over there. We would walk through that area when I had to go to church, and I would say 'Hi' to who was there. I would ask how they were and how they were doing. They would be scrubbing floors and I would say, 'You poor girl.' I know because I was there too. I would start crying when everybody went past me when I was there.

When I was there some girls would sneak down just to see me. They would stand on the side of the wall outside the ward and talk to me from the window. When I knew someone was coming or I heard their footsteps I would tell them to go.

When you were sent to G the only thing you were allowed was what was right there. We were there with the low grades. That's what they called them, low grades. It was another name for severely retarded people. The attendants called them that.

The first thing they had me do when I first arrived was to clean out the toilets. Then I had to shower some of the girls and dress them. We had to scrub the floors on our hands and knees.

When I first arrived there and saw all the people, I thought, 'Oh, no. What am I getting into now? What's going to happen?' There are all these people just sitting around and rocking back and forth and back and forth. Some of them were pulling their hair and eating it. One was in a straitjacket. They had to keep her in it because she hurt other people. They were just sitting there looking at their hands and twirling them around. I knew that it was a place for punishments and I told myself that I wasn't going to stay there and live there. I was glad about that, because I don't think I would have been able to live there. Those people were really bad. Some of them were mean in their ways and in their mind. We slept right between two of them. They always made sure, when you were punished, that you slept with them. There was another girl from another ward that was down there when I was first there, so we talked. But if we got caught we were in trouble. We used to say that we couldn't wait till we got back to the ward. She told me which attendants were mean to watch out for, but we never got a chance to talk about too much.

Whenever we had medication they would line us up and they gave it to us down there too. They took us down to the cafeteria with them, and part of the punishment was we had to eat their ground food. They ground your meat and everything. They piled the stuff right up too. That was what they ate, so you had to, too. I got sick and threw up. It was awful, it was nasty-tasting stuff. They asked me what was wrong. I told them that I didn't like it. They told me that I had to eat it because I was being punished. One time the attendant turned her back and I slopped the ground meat into one of the low grade's trays and told her to eat it. I thought that was funny. She just gobbled it right down.

There were two working girls on the ward in G, plus the girls they were punishing. Working girls had to make sure that there were clothes for each patient and that they were always clean and kept neat. They lived right on the ward and when there was no punishment girls they had to do all the work. After a while I guess they got used to it. They didn't have to eat that ground food. They could go to the movies and walk around the grounds, but life on that ward was bad.

I must have been twelve when I first went on to G. On G–6 we had to wear this combination outfit. The undershirt and the panties came all the way down to your thighs, and then you had on old ladies' stockings. Those dark dreary-looking things. They had these dopey-looking dresses down to your feet. On G, all they did all day was sit there in the day room with the TV on, rocking and making noises and all kinds of things. Some of them would strip themselves and just sit there and the attendants would yell out, 'One of you working girls come out here and take care of this girl. Get those clothes back on her.'

One girl had a straitjacket on all the time because she was going around pulling people's hair.

We had a lot of messers on that ward. Mostly they would do it in their clothes and then we had to clean them. I hated to do that. We had to clean the mess if they went on the floor. I hated it. Who wants to clean someone's rear end at that age? I wouldn't mind cleaning a baby's behind, but not them.

I started treating them kind of mean because I felt if it wasn't for them I wouldn't be there cleaning them. I would throw them on the toilet. I would say, 'Sit there,' and when I got them in the shower I would turn the cold right on them. Sometimes they would start squealing and the attendant would come running and ask what I was doing. I would say, 'Oh, nothing. She caught her toe in the drain.' I was mad. I said, 'If it wasn't for you I wouldn't be here doing this junk.'

Some of them on G were more intelligent than they looked. Some of them, if you would hit them, they would hit you right back. I didn't think that would happen. One time I hit one of the patients because she really got on my nerves. I told her to sit down on that toilet. She wouldn't. She got up. By the time she got out the door she had messed. I could have killed her. I slapped her. I slapped the hell out of her. I was so mad. The attendants were out in the day room, sitting by the desk, watching TV. The attendants didn't do any work. All they did was to give medication and put out clean clothes. They wouldn't dress them or anything. It was up to us to do that. We were the ones that had to go struggling to put them on the toilets. You had to drag them by the arms. In front of the attendants you had to be really nice. You couldn't be mean, but when they weren't in sight you could give it to them.

One time I hit a low-grade girl and almost got into trouble. She just looked at me. She got mad and started having one of her little spells or a temper tantrum. The attendants came running and said 'What's wrong?' I said, 'Oh, I don't know. I tried to get her on this toilet and she won't sit down.' So I got out of it. If they found out, you were in trouble.

The other time I got put in a straitjacket on G was in the shower. There was one of the low grades that I didn't care for. She hit me when I was washing her. I told this working girl that I wasn't going to wash her. I told her to let the other girl wash her – I wasn't. She told me that I gotta do it. I said, 'Well, I am not doing it.' I pushed that low grade out of the shower and told her, 'You get out of here. I'm not doing you.' The attendant went and told the head boss, and that's when they put me in the strait-jacket. I liked being in it because I didn't have to do anything.

I didn't think about them low grades being in the same institu-tion as me. I really didn't think about anything. I just knew I was there and I was going to live there for a while. Maybe never get out. I thought I was going to be there until I was in my rocking chair. Maybe die there – but it didn't happen.

The people in G were retarded but those in O Building were just slow learners. We were really just slow learners. That's what I was. To me that was not retardation at all. To me slow learner is the proper word for it. Most of them in O were there because of problems – home problems, problems with school. In our ward, people had problems getting along. They needed some kind of professional help – not that they got any at Empire. You had to be kidding to say they got any help there. By professional help what I mean is getting good schooling. Being taught. Being able to be understood by other people. They didn't get that, so I call what we got as unprofessional help.

They called it a training school. Now they call it a develop-mental center. Those names don't hit no bell. Developmental sounded to me like they were really trying to get kids developed. That's not what really goes on there. They try to make a name for it, but the names they are using is not what they are doing at all. They should name it for what they are doing, but they don't want anybody to know. I would name it 'prison.' A prison home. That is really what it was. The bad treatment that they were giving us. Developmental center – boy, they have a lot of nerve. That name don't ring no bell. The administration, they try to hide like they don't know anything.

Without the director's permission, how could they do all that they were doing? I know that the director must know something about it because that is what makes the school – the director. The director died some time ago. Boy, he was a mean son of a bitch. I have seen him face to face, but I never seen him in action. Boy, just the stuff that went on in that school. I knew that he was no good – no good at all.

People get to Empire because there was no place to go. Their parents just rejected them, or said, 'Look, I am not going to take time to take care of these kids.' That's what happened to a lot of the kids – the ones on G, too. The mothers couldn't stand their kids having big heads, or no legs, and they were upset about it, and threw them in the school. That's what especially happened with the little kids in X Building.

When I first went on to the ward everything was pretty good. Then I started getting very bad. After a while I was on a lot of Thorazine – 250 milligrams, it was. I didn't like some of the kids and certain attendants either. Some were meaner than others and some were just plain rotten. I didn't like some of the punishments that they did and I reacted to that. I think that's when I really started getting bad. At times I felt that I needed punishment. Then there were times that I wasn't doing anything that bad. If they punished me when I didn't think I was bad, that is when the temper tantrums would really start. I would just stand there and get upset and start cursing and swearing and throwing things around. Anything that was in my reach I would throw – I didn't care what it was. It was the way people were treating me that caused it. Once they gave me a hypo of Thorazine. It knocked me right out. I fell asleep in the day room. That needle went in and I started screaming and then I fell right out. The nurse told me it was going to be good for me.

After a while I started getting visits, maybe once a month, from my mom and my father – my stepmother, I should say. He was living with her in Johnstown. Things started getting a little bit better. I was able to go out during the afternoon, and eat or go for a ride with them.

Christmas wasn't much at Empire. There was just a tree, and I think whoever stayed on the ward got a gift. Not everybody went home. I don't think that I spent one Christmas there in the four years I was there.

While I was at Empire, my real father and stepmother visited. I think once my real mother came. My stepfather worked at Cornerstone State School for twelve years. He delivered the bakery goods from Cornerstone to Empire on a truck. I knew what time that truck came around and I would be up at the window to see him. He would wave up to me. If I was out in the playground, he would pull over and stop and talk. I would ask him about my mother and stuff. I felt good because I was special at the time, you know. I was the only person on the grounds that had a father that came around in a truck and could stop and talk to me. The attendants knew my stepfather and they never said anything about him stopping. In fact, if I wanted to get in the truck and sit with him they wouldn't say anything. He didn't come every day. If he did they probably would have not thought about it the same way. People get jealous and stuff.

My real father came regularly and took me home on Easter, Christmas, and Thanksgiving. He was a drinker. So what? He would come. Drunk or no drunk, he was there.

I saw my stepmother then, too. It was a pretty good relationship until I started going for longer visits. Then I got jealous and we never really had a relationship. I felt that if my stepmother could come and take me home, and my own mother couldn't, there was something wrong. I thought that she didn't really care.

She was glad that I was just dumped somewhere to get me out of her hands. That is what was going through my mind.

At the state school, if you were bad or if you had a cold, they would not let you go home for a visit. It was up to the doctor. I got punished once or twice. This one time they never even called my parents to tell them that I couldn't come and not to get me. They came all the way up there to Empire and found out that I couldn't go. My father was furious. They let me go down and have a couple of minutes to visit and kiss them goodbye. Boy, that hurt me. I went to the ward and cried.

The best time at Empire was when I knew I was being transferred to Cornerstone State School. The doctor and everybody on my ward thought it would be good for me to have more freedom. I was improving and stuff and showing that I was able to do things. My parents were visiting and I was acting better.

Cornerstone State School

It was the fall of 1969 when I left Empire. I'm not sure why, but the doctor came and said, 'Pat, we are going to transfer you.' The next thing I knew they were processing my papers. I think it was in February or the last part of January that I was getting packed. I moved in February.

I had no idea why I was being transferred. No one told me. One fact was mentioned – that this place had more freedom. I didn't know where I was going. My attendant told me I was heading to the Cornerstone.

The bus was stacked full. I mean, people were sitting on people's laps just to get them all in. There were different people from different buildings – not just ours.

I felt good about going – good because I didn't want to stay there. I didn't like it. I thought it would be better. No more strait-jackets.

I was fifteen or sixteen then. I remember the bus ride. I was thinking, 'Where am I going? What kind of place? Would it be better? Would it be nicer? Would the people be better? Would the kids be better? Would I make friends? Would it be something like I had to go through when I went to Empire?'

When we got there, we walked into two double doors to a carpeted place called the business office. The office is on the side. We just sat down and they took us down to the cafeteria to have lunch. It was a brick building – not a prison; it wasn't like that. It was not as old as Empire, but it was old looking. It needed some fixing, like painting and stuff. We didn't line up as much. Only when we went to the cafeteria, so that everybody wouldn't be rushing for the food. We had to sleep in one big dormitory.

I was put on the ward with the elderly people. I stayed there around a week or two. Then I went to A–6. That was for girls. They were all about my age. I stayed there until I went to the halfway-house colony.[3] I went to Colony House, 631–632 Main Street. Then to a family care home, then back to the state school again. Only when I went back to the state school it was new, they ripped down the old one.

I was on the ward from about age fifteen or sixteen to about seventeen. This was in the old building. That is where I lived when I got there.

There were about twenty-four on my ward. I don't know how many of them were homosexual. I don't think too many, because a lot of them had their own pleasures in other areas when they had free time – with the males. Some of the girls were afraid and some weren't. Some were afraid to meet males because they

---

3 Many institutions once operated 'colonies' for higher-functioning residents. These colonies typically were designed to be economically self-sufficient through residents' labor – farming or industrial work. By today, colonies have either been closed or converted into (or at least redesignated as) 'group homes.'

hadn't had the opportunity before, so they realized that girls were girls and maybe they could get better satisfied that way. I don't know – there is a lot of it like that. None of those girls tried to get to me, because they knew that I was very serious. Bessie said that I was very serious even when she tried to joke with me. I didn't catch on to her jokes. I just didn't laugh because I didn't think they were funny. She said, 'You are not the joking type, are you?' I said, 'No, I am very serious, in fact.' They knew that I was serious, and that I was not going to be doing those kinds of things. So I didn't do it and they wouldn't come up and ask. I didn't fully understand things like that, but I knew better not to go do it with some other girl.

I thought those girls were dirty. To me that is dirty, because you don't have to do it with a female. There are many males that are willing to do it. I never told on them, though. I was afraid that they would beat me up. I saw them beat another girl up for telling – they did it in the bathroom. Once they pulled my hair and spit on me.

Some of the girls were tougher than others. Some were afraid of others. They did things and acted like they were God Almighty. You were just nothing and you were just no good and so you better watch out for them. A couple of them hung out together. They were mostly the people that thought that they could run the ward.

One night I woke up and I looked down and there were these girls going at it under the bed. They were doing everything. It was just like what you would do with a male only they did it a little different. Some of the girls that did that, I think they were afraid. They haven't had time to learn about males. They are not sure about themselves and are afraid that they are not able to make connections or satisfy the partner. They were taught to be proper, so they are afraid of males, so what else can they do but satisfy their feelings some other way? Also they didn't have to get examined for pregnancy.

Some of these homosexual girls didn't wait until night. They did it right there on the ward. They didn't care. We had a clothes room. They would take that clothes room and go in there and pull coats down and stuff like that. Sometimes they got caught and sometimes they didn't.

After the girls who were homosexual came back from Special Treatment after a couple of days, it was like the whole thing was forgotten. Special Treatment was a special place with lockup rooms – to keep you away from everybody and to punish you. Nobody talked about it until it happened again. It wasn't a freak-like thing. I guess it was just to meet their own needs and satisfaction.

There were many times I got upset on the ward. The attendants and I had a couple of rounds. The tough girls sat there and laughed. Some even joined in the arguments. They would egg us on – just to get things going. They liked to have a free brawl to watch. They would call the patrolmen in to settle the girls down. I remember one of the girls, she had a seizure in her sleep and died. They came down then, too.

I had this one fight with one of the tough girls. I ripped her clothes almost off – you know, stripped. We got each other on the floor and I rapped her head on a chair leg. I beat her face with my fists so hard. I punched her in the stomach and I kicked her with my shoe. I almost gouged her eyes out with my nails. I had long nails for a while. She got some good scratches on my face and body, too. I said, 'This will teach you a lesson. You better leave me alone the next time.' She got up and said, 'Help.' I felt pretty good. I felt big. I started becoming a bully myself. I was sick and tired of people just beating me all the time. I told myself, 'I am not going to take this shit anymore.'

I would say that I went to Special Treatment three or four times. Not all for fighting. Some was for getting into deep arguments with attendants. I threatened them a lot. They were superior over me, that's what they thought, they thought they could do anything that they wanted. I felt that the only way I could get anything was by threatening people. I figured that if I couldn't do physical hurt to them, maybe I could scare them. Once I threatened one that I would take a knife from the kitchen and kill her. One time I really pulled the table in the dining room over and dumped the food on the floor. It was when one of the attendants told me I couldn't go to a dance. I said to myself, 'That's OK. I will fix you.' The kids egged me on. 'Come on Pattie. Let's get something going.' They always used me. I was always willing to do something stupid to get myself in trouble. I would always get the dirty end of it. When I tipped the table over, I laughed. I got punished. That was not too funny. That was not the only time I pushed a table over.

When we lined up for meals there were always too many people that wanted to be first. They wanted to crowd. Then there was this lady who worked there that used to just slop my food and the other kids' food on our plates. It was like I was a pig or something. I didn't like that. Once I just took my tray and threw it right at her. It went all over her uniform. I said, 'Don't ever slop my food on my tray like that again. I am not an animal.' I got really angry. There was people sitting there in a row. I just turned the table and then I did it to the one next to it. The attendants had to run. They were afraid. They didn't know what to do. They called the patrolmen and they kind of blocked me with their arms. They put my arms in back of me to calm me down. They just talked. They took me to a separate room upstairs in the office where I went when I first got there – when I was admitted. They talked to me but they didn't hurt me. They said that they understood that I was emotionally upset and that I needed help. That's when they started putting me on medication.

People nagged me. That is why, nowadays, when people start telling me things like, 'You are not going to go here,' or, 'You are not going there,' 'Do this. Do that,' I just start thinking about

144   those days. Sometimes I have a reaction to it. In the last couple of years – or year – I think I am better. I have learned to control a lot of my anxieties and emotional problems.

I remember once I was at STA[4] and I ripped an attendant's uniform because she bothered me when I was upset. She came in and started teasing me. She said that I was going to stay in there another day 'cause she was going to tell the doctor. See, I had to go to the bathroom real bad and she wouldn't let me out, so I wet the floor there in my room. I told her, 'It's your own fault.' She told me that I knew that there were only certain times that people could go. She told me that she was going to tell the doctor and get me to stay there another couple of days. I went nuts. I went back and forth in my room screaming and banging on the walls, saying, 'I want my father and mother.' She got her uniform torn and it was her own fault.

See, it was isolation – STA. It had the steel doors with a little tiny window that you can just peek into to see what is going on. They had a key to it that they could open and shut.

There were other ways that the attendants treated us like animals. When they put us in isolation it was like being an animal. I don't think that I would have gone really crazy, like banging my head against the wall, if I wasn't put in STA isolation. I really didn't do anything so criminal to be isolated like that. They just threw me in there like an animal. 'OK, doggie, into your room. Hang it up and forget about you.' They just talked to you when it was time to go to bed and to feed you.

There was this steel tray that they put in there. They gave you a great big tablespoon – no fork and knife. They just pushed it in the door and said, 'There, now you eat.' They were afraid to bring your food in because if you were mad you would throw it at them. I had one incident when I did that. There was a lady who came in and said, 'Here is your lunch.' She was so sweet and everything. She had been bothering me all day. She sat there

4 Special Treatment Area.

by the door saying, 'You'll get out some day. Just be good.' I
didn't want to hear that. She was like tormenting me. Then she
came in with the food and said, 'You cute thing. Why are you so
bad?' I said, 'I got a surprise for you.' I threw the food all over
her face and clothes. Mrs Reilly, the charge, came in and sent the
other one home because she was such a mess. See, they thought
that because I was locked up they could do anything that they
wanted. That is one day when I went crazy – I mean, I almost
went crazy. I was going back and forth. I was flinging my hands
up against the wall. I was calling out for my father, 'I just need
you. Come on, take me home.' I cried and screamed. My throat
was so sore all night because of that. I was just screaming and
crying. I just wanted to kill. I had all this anxiety. If she would
have come in again I probably would have strangled her.

And that was just from being isolated. Away from everybody
in a bare room, a small room with no area to move. You walk
around because there is nothing else to do. You would finally
just sit there on the floor and fall asleep or bang on the walls.
'Let me out of here. Let me out of here.' I didn't go berserk, but I
went through something. I was close, very close. I screamed and
cried and banged the door.

The doctors had to sign the papers saying you had to be put in
Special Treatment Area. I don't call them doctors. I call them
psychiatrists. Not even that. They think they know their business, but they really don't. If a person that is not really doing
anything that can be called criminal is locked up behind steel
doors, that doesn't tell me that the doctors that do it are very
smart. Why should you stick someone in an isolated room when
all she did is get upset or threaten to do something? Threatening
doesn't mean anything. If you go into action that would be
something else. Then they might decide, 'OK. Let's lock her up.'
But they didn't even wait. They just pulled you in and that was
it. I can't really say to this day that they were really doctors. I
think that they were just there for that high money. It is not you
that they care about. If they did, a lot of these things that go on

wouldn't. If they would spend more time, give you more attention. People need attention. They don't need to be pushed here and there and into isolation. They need the time of people. They need to be taught different things about outside living. They knew that we were not going to stay there forever – maybe they thought that we were, but we knew that we weren't. We were bad, but everybody is. We are all human.

The attendants they came in day after day and were mean to us. They were snappy. They had their days of being upset, so why can't they expect us to have our days? They would come in and say, 'Oh, my husband, we just didn't get along last night. He is just on my nerves. I can't take it another minute. Stay out of my way. Try to be good today.' We would just act up. It told us that this woman was frustrated and upset and mad. Why should we behave for her when she doesn't try to help us? We gave her her own medicine. We did. Just snap right back at her. We just show them that they don't take us into consideration, then we don't take them into consideration.

They don't call them attendants now. They call them therapy aides. That sounds pretty fake. I wonder what kind of therapy they are giving. They probably are still strangling and throwing kids against the wall. I don't know – they need some training. They have to learn that we are human, too.

We were always thinking about the attendants, too. 'You are only here for the money. You don't care about us.' They would say, 'If we didn't care, dear children, we wouldn't be here.' They would just sit around and wouldn't take any time to teach us anything. They would get around this little round table and talk and talk with their feet up on the chair, smoking. They would tell us, 'I am going to relax today, children. Have a good time. Go about your business.' That is just not the way to run a school and to make children happy.

At the old school we had dances. The business club set them up. We would plan for weeks and make up the invitations. I remem-

ber they had colored lights at the dance. They would make you
dance wild. With the music going and everything – we had a
good time. They had like a raffle, and they would choose the
king and queen and put a crown on the top of their head. They
would put numbers in a bag and have people pick. The winner
got a stuffed animal and became king. There were king and
queen chairs. They had velvet on them and signs saying King
and Queen. It was really nice. One time we took a vote who we
wanted. There was this couple that had been going together for
about a year that got it. That was all exciting because it meant
something to us.

Everybody has problems. There is no one perfect in this world. I
don't care if you are in an institution or outside. As far as I am
concerned I got treated pretty bad at Empire. They wouldn't let
me make up my mind half the time about what I wanted to do. I
proved them a lot of points, that I was able to do a lot of things.
In fact when I was cleaning all the time at Cornerstone, if I
wasn't able why did they send me up and let me help bathe and
feed the children?

They gave me the work to more or less get me off the ward.
Sometimes the people on my ward would bother me. I didn't get
along with a few people. Some of the attendants would say, 'OK,
Pat. Why don't you go up and see if you can do something with
the little kids. Help out Mrs Bates.' I would say, 'OK.' I would go
up there and help. It made me feel a lot better. It made me feel
worthwhile – something beside sitting in the dumb day room
and looking at TV like the rest of those dumb-dumbs.

I was always a hard worker. I didn't have to worry about that.
There are many times that they would just sit down and let Pattie do it. They would sit around talking and smoking. If you
didn't do it, they would call you lazy. Maybe for a minute or so I
would sit down and have a break. But I was afraid that they
would call me lazy. Even though you would work hard for the
attendants, they would tell the other attendants that you didn't

do anything, just to start gossip. There was a lot of gossip at the school. They would get together on breaks or during lunch and say I wasn't a hard worker. Sometimes they would call you 'stupid' and 'dummy.' The kids would get me angry sometimes and I would yell. I was supposed to be crazy because I was raising my voice.

I had a fight with Mrs O'Brien once. She said to me, 'You know, you are dumb sometimes.' I told her that that wasn't true, that it is just that I have my ways and you have yours. That started a big fight. I told her, 'I work my butt off all the time and you have all this bad stuff to say about me. I don't want to go up there and work anymore.' Finally, I just told her to bug off. I told her to leave me alone. I just wanted to be by myself. She says, 'No. I want to talk to you.' Then that started it. I really got going. I couldn't help it. I got carried away and hit her. Then she reacted with a broom. She hit me with the handle. I felt like I was an animal.

I got really upset with one of the attendants one day. They set this Angela Smith – a resident – on me. They couldn't handle me so they set her on me. We had a fight and were pulling at each other's hair. They wanted me to go outside and play. I wanted to watch TV. I wouldn't get up. So they picked out Angela. She came over to me and said, 'Why don't you leave the attendants alone?' Then she jumped right on me and started grabbing for my hair and clothes. She ripped my clothes. She was a black girl and had short hair. I pulled that good. I got her on the floor and punched her in the stomach. I said, 'You will learn to keep your hands off me, girl. You don't have any right to be doing this. You are a resident.' She started yelling, 'Help, help me.' I thought, 'Oh, Pattie, you are the bravest girl there.' I felt so good.

I had another fight about going out. This time it was with a man attendant. I raised my voice to him. I told him to something himself. He grabbed hold of me and threw me. He was a big bully. I went right back after him. I tore his shirt and he pulled my hair good. There must have been a couple of handsful of my hair. He sent me to my room and told me not to come out. I told one of the girls to bring a record. I put it on as loud as I could. I figured I'd fix him.

They moved that guy down to the old ladies' ward. I went up and told Dr Miller about it and took my hair up there that he pulled out to show him. I fixed him good. I told him, 'He can't do some of the things that he does to the young kids. I didn't want to go outside. I wasn't feeling good.' He said, 'Pat, we all got to go according to the rules.' I told him that I realized that, but when someone doesn't feel good they got to realize that we are human, too. The guy blew up. I mean he was angry. He said, 'This girl ought to be put away somewhere, because she is really dangerous. She attacked me.' They put him away.

I believe this way about attendants. They are human beings. Everyone is a human being. They don't realize that us kids have emotional problems. They don't realize what we have gone through. They don't realize where we come from. We didn't have moms or dads to straighten us out when we were kids. They don't realize all this stuff. I am sure they don't or they wouldn't act this way towards us. That is the only way I can think of it. They were good. They had their good points too. I got along with that guy I had the fight with good before that mishap. He should have made it easier on me. I didn't have to go outside.

Attendants don't really care about your feelings. 'I am an attendant and you listen to me. I am your boss.' Pattie was not going to stand for that.

I was on medication in Empire. I don't remember from Empire to Cornerstone – how long it was after I got to Cornerstone that they put me back on. I do recall it was Dr Zola who was the one who put me back on. She started me off on a little green pill, then a tan pill, then it was something else. My stepfather knew about it and didn't like it. He said, 'This girl doesn't need to be doped. What she needs is someone to show her that they care. Doping her just makes her quiet and out of your hair.' He went to Dr

Zola about it. She called down to the ward and got me up there. He told her how when I went home on vacation I didn't have any medication and I was doing fine. My father told them that he didn't want me on medication any more. He meant business. He was going to tell the director.

It's hard keeping straight in my head all the things that happened when I was at Cornerstone State School. See, I was there for a while and then I went out into a colony and then to foster care and then I came back. It is terrible to live in a place like that. Some of the people who lived there were really gone – not like you and me. You pitied them because they were deformed – they were people that couldn't help themselves. The babies with legs wrapped around their heads. They were born like that. Babies with big tubes in their heads draining out water. It made your heart bleed.

In Search of My Family

My mother started seeing me. I was closer and she could travel. She could have traveled to Empire if she cared. I remember the first time she came to visit me. It was on my birthday. I got a card and a paper doll. She always treated me like a little girl. Like when I was thirteen and she was still giving me dolls. I was getting older and I wasn't looking for dolls. My stepfather was the one that mentioned it to her, that she can't be treating me like a little girl all my life. I wasn't with her when I was little so she wanted to try and make up for it.

When she first came to Cornerstone, I felt rejected. I started to get better. She would say, 'Give mommy a kiss.' I wouldn't even give her a kiss. I would turn away.

My stepfather worked there so he had to come up on the ward with the carts. He would stop on his way with the goods. I used to holler out, 'Hi, Dad, how is mom?' Boy, that felt great. I was special. He would say, 'How would you like to come home this weekend?' So it kind of switched from my real father to my stepfather. I loved him but I still cared for my real father.

The first day I visited my mother's house was something. I was very quiet at first. I sat there and just tried to make myself at home. Later on in the evening I opened up and started talking. It was real hard at first because I didn't realize that she was *really* my mother. She hadn't come around. She hadn't seen me, and there she was trying to tell me that she was my mother. I couldn't really believe that, because she hadn't seen me when I was a baby.

I did have some trouble when they took me off medicine and I was at my mother's, but that was because she gave me medicine. I remember that night home, it was one of my first visits. It was Friday, because that is the night my father bowls, so he wasn't there. My little sister was four years old then and my other brother was there, my stepbrother was seven years old, and then there was one going on nine. My stepsister, who is about sixteen, was there, too – well, they were all home. My mother said, 'Don't you think that it is time for a little medicine?' I guess she thought I was getting really fidgety and nervous. She said that I should take this pill, 'We don't have to tell them – just take it – I think it will do you good.' I think that she had some old medicine that I took and she kept it home just in case. She gave me one and I just started really getting upset.

I can't recall what exactly happened. I was really getting bad. Everything that she said kind of ticked me off. I was walking into the kitchen and she told me that I didn't turn my head or anything. My eyes were just straight. I was just going like a robot. She said that I went into the drawer and took out a knife and sliced her. I don't believe that either. She couldn't show me the scar. She tried to tell me that I tried to smother my little sister with a pillow and I don't recall that either. She called my stepfather home from bowling right in the midst of everything and told him what was going on. He had to come home and restrain me – hold me down on the floor. I was really going at it. She was crying and that's when I came out of it. After he had pinned me down, I was OK. He let me back up and asked me what had happened. I said, 'I don't recall.' I had looked forward to a visit with my mother – I never dreamed anything like that would happen.

At that time my mother's house wasn't as pretty as it is now. It is all paneled and the kitchen is remodeled. Jim, my stepfather, won a $10,000 lottery ticket. His picture was in the paper with his daughter and mom holding it with a big smile. I didn't get a pretty penny out of that either. I feel kind of bad about that, but the kids got a brand new swing set and sandbox, and the back-yard was all fenced. My stepfather remodeled the whole kitchen for her. Wall-to-wall carpeting and new bathroom and bedroom set and a new car – a '74 Duster – brown. The organ that she has now she got after my stepfather died. A $4,000 organ. It is like a horseshoe. It's got three rows of keys and all these beautiful little buttons that she can push. She has got clothes. Man, don't talk about clothes. I hate to talk about it. Her long dresses, long with slits up the side. That woman has got it.

I knew my stepfather better than my mother because I always saw him down at Empire. After the drug thing I went home regular – see they knew that that was a trance. I went home every other weekend except when I was punished and wrote up in the book.

At first my visits with my mother were good, but then she started telling me that everything that happened to me was dad's fault. She told me that if she could have kept me as a baby she would have made a good life for me. She told me that she tried so hard to get me back. That's a damn lie, too. She never even tried. My father was drinking so much that he didn't care if we came home or not. One time I brought up why she and dad weren't together. I said, 'Why can't you, dad, and I have just been a happy family and be like normal people?' She said, 'Honey, it will never happen.' You know, around 1974, she met my father somewhere and they went out on a hot date. Now, how do you like that? I found out through one of her close friends. She told me after she went out. It is really hard for me to understand.

It's funny, when I was visiting home with my mother I would fight with her. Like she would ask me to do the dishes and I would give her trouble, but when my stepfather was home I was an angel. I would sit on the couch, quiet – I wouldn't do any-thing. I don't know, it is something about males. When they were around, I was just quiet. I don't know if I worry about them punishing more. When there is females around, it is a different story. I step on more females than I do males. It was the same thing at the state school. When there was a male attendant on the ward, I acted different. That's true except for that one I told you about who wanted me to go outside. They are stronger than females and they could hurt me if they wanted.

I felt abnormal because I wasn't living with my family. I felt abnormal because I was at the state school. I felt abnormal – like I wouldn't play with the other kids and go outside for walks. It didn't feel like I was crazy – just abnormal. I felt that I just wasn't like other people.

It was about after one year of visiting that things got real bad. When she slapped me, I told her, 'You know, Mom, you didn't raise me so you don't have the right to slap me. I am not really home, I am just visiting.' We really hurt each other and I just got tired of it. The most harmful thing I could say to her was, 'You didn't raise me and you're no good because you didn't bring me into this world and a regular family.' That really hurt her. She would break down because she knew that was the truth. I could call her names, but saying that is what really hurt. She couldn't rub that off because of that was in her heart and that was lost for her life. That is why we don't have any relationship now. It is because we deeply hurt each other over what had happened.

There was a time when we really got into it and she said, 'You know, honey, sometimes I wish that you were one of my miscar-riages. I wouldn't have to go through all of this.' She said that what happened wasn't her fault. It was my fault and my father's. I said, 'You brought me into this world, didn't you?' She said, 'Your sister isn't like this.' I said, 'Well, the truth is that you loved my sister more than you did me.' She wouldn't admit it, but I know she does. She always babied my sister more – before she got married she could come home any time she wanted and go for a ride in the car. That's my sister that's in Oregon now. I guess I always felt rejected because my sister got the best care and I was like no good. Ever since the day she told me that she wished that I was one of her miscarriages – that was the end. She said that about a year ago. People say, 'Why don't you call up your mom and talk to her?' No, I don't want to know anything about her.

When I was at Cornerstone, the doctors arranged so that I was visiting my real father and my real mother at the same time. I was taking turns. I would go to my father's and dad would say, 'How was it with mom?' We were going back and forth, and finally I said to mom, 'I can't take this any more. It's either got to be you or him.' I felt that I couldn't choose one or the other because I felt it would hurt one of them. I was just worried about everybody else, but not myself. Then I did start visiting mom more than I did dad – I didn't think mom would be rejected any more. I just wanted to be loved, loved, loved.

I guess when I started visiting I accepted a lot of her good deeds and covered up my feelings about her mistakes. When I was seventeen, it got different. I covered up what my life was and tried to be nice and good, but at seventeen I started opening up my mouth more. I started thinking, 'Why am I in this school, how come this happened to me, why can't I be like other kids out in the world?' I started opening up to every fact of my life. Why, why, why? I wanted an answer. At eighteen and nineteen, things really crashed. Mom didn't want no part of me and I didn't want no part of her. She is afraid of me now. I know that she is. She should have let me come home when I was deadly hurt.

Once I took care of my mother when she was sick. She was deadly sick with varicose veins. Lying on the couch with them bloated right out of her legs – they looked like they were going to pop any minute. I hot-packed her legs and took care of her. I put the kids to bed and did good deeds.

When I called her this January, she said, 'Honey, I don't have time to talk to you.' I said, 'If you don't have time now you never will.' She hung up before I could even say anything more. That hurt, that really hurt.

My mother said it was dad's fault. It was my fault because I brought more pressure into her life. She said that I had it better than she had it. I told her that while she was at home having all those babies out of wedlock I was off rotting in that school. If I were to have a baby out of wedlock I would expect my mother to be very angry. I wouldn't tell her, because it is not her business. If I brought her the baby and said, 'Here is your grandchild,' she would say, 'Where is the man, honey?' I would say, 'I don't have one.' She would say, 'Well, don't bring it here. It is a disgrace.' She would reject me. I know she would.

One time she sat down and said, 'Honey, you know I have been thinking. You and I should talk. You're older now and able to understand.' So we started to talk and I asked her, 'Why did I have to go through the torment and the torture I did? Why couldn't it have worked out?' She said, 'Well, honey, this is teaching you a lesson for when you get married. This might happen to you and your child.' I thought, 'God help me.' If anybody ever touches or tries to take my child away there'll be trouble. We will get by any way we can. He will have enough clothes to keep him warm and enough food in his belly. I will see to that – if it means going to somebody's house and eating, he will have food. No one is going to take my child. That's all there is to it. It won't happen.

She told me that the reason I was sent away to those schools was that I had emotional problems. If I didn't get special treatment I wouldn't be able to function in life. She said later in her life she was seeing a daughter that was going to be a tough kid to take care of, so she thought that I better get settled down now to get ready for future life. You should never take someone's life like that and see into the future. You should never say that I see in the future this girl with sixteen babies or something like that. I see this girl running around being a whore. That is unfair. She said that she saw I was going to have problems so she wanted to do something. What I needed was to stay home instead of being put through all that torment.

At Cornerstone State School I was closer to my dad, too. I mean right there in the city. It was a lot easier for me to go. I had a father and a stepmother to go home to when Christmas came. I had somebody that gave me gifts. I made gifts in crafts and gave them. I couldn't buy, because I didn't have the money. I did feel a lot warmer and a lot closer and a lot happier then.

I always felt bad about not having family. When you are younger you look for a family to want you. I looked all the time. Even now I want people to want me. I don't know if I want to live with a family now. I am older and like to have my own place. I want to go to the movies when I want and come in when I want, watch TV when I want, and listen to the radio. I don't want someone to come in and say, 'OK. Now we are going to watch TV everybody.' I eat whenever I want, if it means three, four, five, six times a day. You can't do that in a family.

I did tell you about my stepmother. We got along fine until I went for a long week. When I was there I would get kind of nervous and upset. Things started bothering me and we would have arguments. We would get to hurting each other, too.

My stepfather died and my real father stopped seeing me. It was after Easter when I was sixteen years old. We got into an argument. He went out drinking. He goes out on weekends and drinks. My stepmother told me to do the dishes. I didn't want to.

I was just tired and I wanted to rest for a few minutes. She told
my father, which she should never have done. He took hold of
me and said, 'How come you didn't do what she told you. How
come?' He threw me on the living-room floor and beat me up.
He slapped me in the face and punched me in the stomach. I
screamed at him – swearing at him and told him to leave me
alone and get away from me. I told him I didn't love him any
more. She took me back to the school because I told her to.

When I got back to Cornerstone, I told the attendants that I
wasn't feeling good – that my stomach hurt and I couldn't eat.
They took me to the doctor and he examined me. He found that
my father had hurt the inside wall of my stomach.

I never went back to my father's after that. It was the same
thing over again – no one cared. I was visiting them all the time
and things were going fine. All of a sudden, nothing – I just
didn't care anymore. He told the doctors that they should put me
in Grand River Reformatory for Girls because I was so bad. I
really wasn't. The doctor told him that I was improving and they
didn't feel that I should go.

Sojourns

I stopped going out to anyone's house. Then they got the idea to
send me to one of their colony houses. They call them halfway
houses but there's nothing new or anything. They are places
owned by the state school, in the community, where about
fifteen residents live. There are attendants there and everything,
so it's a lot like the institution.

It is hard for me to get all these years straight. I think it was '74
when they knocked down the old state school and I was in the
colony. I wasn't at the colony too long, maybe four, or five, or six
months. I was about sixteen years old then.

The colony was good but I got bored. I wanted to go out and
get a better job and start life. I was getting older and I thought

about things that I would like to do. I started thinking about dating and having kids. You couldn't date there.

It's funny. I started thinking about having kids. I thought that the only reason you had intercourse was to have children. I didn't know about the pleasure and the feeling and all that stuff. Someone explained to me that it is not just having children that it was for – it was for meeting your needs. Attendants told me that – new ones. We had a sex-education class. But I started thinking about having a baby at the colony. I just wanted something to call my own. I thought, if I have a baby it is mine and I could take care of it.

At the colony, they had us do all the housework and stuff. They said they were getting us ready for outside living. If we wanted to buy something like a record player, we had to go out and do the work to earn it. They would let us go out two or three times a week and do housework for other people and they would pay us for it. We got $10 a day. The people we were cleaning for – the persons whose house we were cleaning – would give us lunch, too, a sandwich or something.

People knew about the people in the colony doing cleaning so they would just call in. The housemother would say that they had just the girl for them. She would tell me that I was going to work for so and so, and such and such a place. Sometimes they would give us all the heavy work, like moving the furniture and scrubbing and waxing floors. Ten dollars doesn't meet the amount of work you would do, especially if they had you cleaning out the basement. Some people were so darn fussy that they would take a little cloth and go along and say, 'You didn't do this,' or, 'You didn't do that.' I got irritable with them – I would try to satisfy them, though. I didn't have any arguments, because I knew it wasn't proper. They took a certain amount out of the money you made to pay for your room and board. You got to keep the rest, say $5 a week for spending money. I usually went out three times a week.

At the colony it was all right. I just didn't think anything of it. It was better than the school – less people, better food. You could cook whatever you wanted sometimes. You all had to sit down to the same meal, but there were times like at snack time you could fix things. We cleaned our own place on Saturday morning and in the afternoon you could do what you wanted.

I didn't like the other girls at the halfway house. Some of them just sat around and didn't make much sense. I didn't want to go any place with them. Some of them were older and had different ideas about things. The oldest was about forty-nine. None of them were really handicapped. There was one that had seizures. Like I said, a lot of them just sat around and watched TV. They were grouchy, especially when they came back from working. I got bored with the housework. I told them that I wanted to be on my own, but they said that I wasn't ready. I would just lie around and go up to my bed. They were shocked one day when I came in to get my stuff to move in with the Bakers.

I think I saw my mother a couple of times when I was at the halfway house. But, like I say, the time of things isn't straight in my head.

In the colony you had to sign in and out when you wanted to go somewhere. When you went to work, you had to sign out in the morning. It was run by the state school, but it was a house to teach girls that come from the school on how to live, how to eat, how to sleep, and how to have a balanced diet.

We had to do our own laundry and cook our own meals. We had to learn how to clean house and different things like that. Some of the girls didn't even know what a vacuum cleaner looked like or how to use it – make their own beds, and clean their own sheets, and fold them, and different things that we had to learn. I already knew all that, but they put me there because that was a place to start and they wanted me to start with everybody else. There would have been a lot of trouble if they didn't have me do what the others had to do. People would be jealous – they were jealous of me already, because I was very alert and I was able to do things they couldn't. They weren't willing to let anybody like me help them.

I think that I got into a lot of fights at the school, too, because people were jealous. Even now, when I see girls from the school and I am looking good, they kind of look mad. That's what happened the other day when I was downtown. I met Mary who had been at the school. I bet she said, 'Look at her. I bet she is whoring around.' She kind of knows the story of my life. She told me that she was getting married. She said, 'I know how to do it right.'

The colony house was right next to a church. Some people from the church came over and asked us if any of us were interested in going. I said I would go and went over one day. I liked it, and the people were very warm and friendly. They took us out to dinner and they started to get to like me. I went on visits to one family's home on weekends. That's how I met the Bakers.

I liked the Bakers. They treated me nice. They asked me if I would like to go home with them and visit and pray. It was better than staying at the halfway house. I didn't think it would hurt me and I thought it would do me a lot of good. I was able to get out and meet with more people. That is what started my growth. From that family on I just met, met, met. I have met so many people now that I know I can't keep up with them. People have realized that Pattie has changed a lot. This isn't a plaything. I am very serious when I talk to somebody about Jesus.

I had Christmas with the Bakers. I brought each of them a gift because I knew if I was going to spend Christmas there, I didn't want to have nothing. They didn't expect me to get them anything, but it wouldn't have been right. I knew she was going to get me something, and I knew that her son was making me something in his art class. I knew that her daughter was making me things. I would feel very out of place and bad if I hadn't. Spending Christmas with them was what started the whole thing. We just kept right on going up until February.

I told her that I didn't like living at the halfway house. So they took me in. I slept in the upper room. It was very nice and cozy. It was a nice family – no hollering, no screaming, nobody nervous. It was just so nice that it was hard to believe. All those years being around people that are screeching and hollering and demanding – that is all you come to know. Everything went fine until April, then all of a sudden I went on a spree. I don't know why. I started getting upset and hollering. I don't know what it was. Even after you are saved by the Lord, that doesn't mean that you are not going to go through your times. I was going through my temptations and trials. The Lord was testing me to see how strong my faith really was – my love for him. I didn't know it.

I just blew up – just started hollering, 'Leave me alone. I don't want nobody. No one cares.' I went through that so many times you would think that I would get over it. Everybody cared, because if they didn't, man, they wouldn't even try. They paid more attention to me than they did their own kids. I can't say that she didn't care, but I don't know, I felt funny. I always wanted my own family. It seems like every time I go through a change moving to a new place, it happens. When I start feeling like calling people mom and dad, something happens. It was a homey atmosphere – like a mom-and-dad place. I just felt that I didn't belong. I started thinking I wanted my own family.

The house was gorgeous. We went every place we wanted – shopping about every day. At the time I wasn't working. I did work a couple of places – at a prescription place. But I couldn't make the change fast enough, so the first night I worked there they fired me. I felt bad about that. I think this did something, too. When you are not working and living with someone it throws you off kilter. I feel, Why do people have to support me? Their kids are out there working. The Bakers didn't get any money from the state school. They were going to, but they never got sent it. They were supposed to give a certain amount each month for room and board, but somehow they still had me as living at the halfway house. So here they were supporting me and me not making anything to give them. They weren't rich, but they had a lot.

Her son was seventeen and the daughter was married and not living at home. She came to visit a lot.

I would get up and eat breakfast and sit around and watch TV. I would volunteer to do the laundry and cleaning. But that is not all there is to life, just cleaning, mopping, and waxing. I was not willing to say, 'OK, this is what I need.' I was always afraid to say anything. I didn't have any way to get around. If I wanted to get a job, I did mention it to her and Bill one night. They suggested jobs for me but we never could go and get them because there was no bus going to the city and Bill had the car. The state school didn't do anything about it. I told them I wanted a job, too, and they knew I was upset about it.

Mrs Baker was good to me. I call it consideration. She showed me she cared. She loved me like her own daughter. She would take her clothes off and give them to me if I didn't have anything.

I had a social worker, but I forget who it was. My experience with social workers hasn't been very good. Like, I would call up and I would tell them that I need to talk to someone about a problem. I could come. Or they would say, 'Come down,' and I would get there and we would just jabber and jabber. When everything was over, they really had nothing to say and nothing to do for me.

I remember getting into it with Vera Todd, a social worker down there. Boy, she was something else. I got into her so bad – yelling. I don't know how many people stood at the door and heard me hollering, but there was quite a few. They heard me hollering at her because she just wouldn't listen. She kept on saying, 'Yeah, Pat. I know all about it. You need help.' I said, 'I don't need help. I just need someone to pay more attention to me. That is what I need.' She was talking about finding me a psychiatrist that I could talk to and all this kind of stuff. I told

her that that was not what I needed. What I needed was someone
to understand me and to do something after they say they will. I
asked for a change over from her. After a meeting they changed
me over to Mark Haines. She just would give you all this fake
talk. He was better. She would just ramble on about me needing
the psychiatrist. I didn't need a psychiatrist and I surely didn't
need her either. She said she didn't think that I should live with
a family. She wanted me to stay at the school. I am not saying she
was all bad. I went out to lunch with her and we talked.

Right after I got upset, a friend of the Bakers was visiting. She
was from North Central and had small children. Mrs Baker was
telling her how I was unhappy there. I wasn't really unhappy.
When you're upset it's hard to act like you're happy even if you
like a place. They started talking about how I would be happy
with taking care of the kids, because they knew I loved kids. So I
took my clothes and went over to stay with them. I thought it
would be better. Every time I go to a new home I find a different
pattern and it's better. The kids were good and I liked them.
They were small and I could babysit and play with them. I took
care of the baby sometimes. I liked it with the new family but,
like always, I got used to it and it got wearing.

I got a job through the Youth Opportunity Center. I've had so
many jobs I can't keep track of them. I was either working at
Memorial Hospital or as a chambermaid. I got there by bus. My
first job was when I was still at the state school – that was at
Dunn Nursing Home. When I went to the halfway house, I still
had the job, but I exploded at one of the head nurses because she
told me to clean up this mess from this lady. I said, 'Not me, get
someone else to do that.' They didn't like that – no way. My job
was training to be a nurse's aide. My job was like making beds
and washing the patients and dressing them and emptying bed-
pans. They wore diapers or something in their pants and you
had to change them. I liked feeding them, dressing them, and
giving them showers, but I didn't like cleaning them. We had to
mark down when they had a BM and take what they call a speci-

men and learn to take temperatures. It was a training program. I was at Dunn three or four months.

After I blew up, my counselor came up and said, 'You know you can't have a job when you blow up at people. You can't have a job now.' I cried, of course. I felt bad after the yelling. I really didn't do anything bad. I just hollered and told them that I wasn't going to do it.

I didn't like the murse or the student nurse. They were too demanding and too bossy. I have had it all my life – people bossing me. I don't need that when I am working, too. I expect it from one or two people, but not everybody pushing me here and there and saying, 'Oh Pat, would you do this?' Pat is always pushed with the dirty work and that is not fair either. I always got all the dirty work. I told them I was fed up with it and that I wasn't doing it no more.

Every time I get a new job I think it's going to be all right. Then, like with a new home, it blows up. People say I am a short-term person. I don't stay with anything long. I don't think that is true, because I proved that I could stay places.

I liked the patients, but I couldn't stand my superiors. I couldn't stand to think that I had so many people over me. I liked the patients because I felt they needed help. If I am going to get that old, I want help some day. I wanted to be the best I could be to them. I never blew up with any of my patients. Some of the supervisors were cruel to the patients. They would pull their hair when they were combing it and get rough. They wouldn't want that if they were in their position. They would leave their patients in the day room in front of the TV in these geriatric chairs – they were like high chairs. They had feet things where you could rest your feet and they would prop them in there with a pillow. Some fell over and slept. They couldn't get out of there. They just left them there with no attention.

Then I worked at Memorial in the kitchen. One of my social workers got that for me. My social worker told me not to blow up again, but I burned up on that one too. That's when I was at the *Murdocks*, the second family. I was taking the bus from North Central City. One day I was dressed clean and neat and had my hair net on. I was ready to go to work. I was down in the locker room. One of the other girls that worked there said to the person next to her, 'Look at that white so-and-so. What is she doing here? She thinks she is great.' I was standing there by my locker when she started with me. I didn't say anything because I was afraid. I walked upstairs and we were doing the trays from the morning service. Mrs Cohen was there. She is this big fat lady who was mean and demanding. She told me to go to the cooler in a mean way. I got the trays from upstairs and loaded them on the cart. I just pushed the cart so hard in the hall and the dishes went over. I was angry with that woman. When I did it I thought it was the funniest thing on earth because I wanted to bother her so bad it wasn't funny. I said to myself, 'I'll fix you.' I did, too, but I fixed myself by getting fired. She started yelling at me and I told her, 'When I come in with a bad mood in the morning, I don't take it out on you. You don't have no right to take your stuff out on me.' I only worked there a month or so.

I didn't even get along with the other girls that worked there. There was this mulatto that was there that we never clicked. We couldn't talk to each other without disagreeing. Once she asked if I wanted to go to a party one night. I told her that I had to go all the way out to North Central City. I didn't feel like going to a party when I couldn't get home. She said I was a party pooper. She started saying I always had a frown, and stuff like that. I'm not the type to wear a smile all the time. She was always picking. Then one time I went down to the locker room to get changed and catch the bus and she threatened me with a knife. She said if I came down there by myself she would get me. It was all over stupid things that I wasn't popular. She must have been angry 'cause I didn't want to go to her party. The other time she brought a book to order Tupperware and told me she wanted me to order some. I didn't have any money. Then there was this guy that she thought wanted to take me out. He was married, but she thought I was trying to steal him from her.

What I was working at these places, I usually made a big mistake. You can make friends by telling people a little about your life. Well, I made enemies by telling them about mine. Right away I would start telling them about the state schools I had been in and the life I had had. They started burning you, so I just don't talk about it to anybody now. You just tell people you can trust – that will keep their mouths shut. You have to tell them you are going to classes or something. The woman I am living with now said that she doesn't want anybody to know about it. It is nobody else's business.

When I first worked at Dunn I wanted people to like me. I told them things and then I got mad once and they said, 'Oh, yeah. Now we know why you get upset – because you don't know how to control yourself.' They would bring it up to my face.

My counselor told me that I shouldn't tell everybody about my life. You would think it would make them sympathetic, but it makes them worse. The woman I am going to live with knows and my pastor. It's hard. Like, people will ask you, 'Where were you a couple of years ago?' I can't say Timbuktu or Ohio when I was never there. They are going to check. Like people in my employment. When you look for a job, they ask, 'What kind of a job did you hold? Where did you live?' and things like that. No use to lie about it to them. They say that is the reason that you get upset, because you was in a school with retarded and crazy people.

Everybody thinks that Cornerstone is for really crazy people. That really hurts. I tell them that there are people there that need more help than others, but it doesn't sink in. That mulatto girl at Memorial told me that she could tell I was from the state school. I don't want to hear stuff like that. I want to forget about it instead of remembering. I call it putting my life in jeopardy when people know about my life and hassle me about it. Then they say I am unhappy all the time. Why shouldn't I be?

I just want to forget about it. Like the pastor says, it's better to forget your past. Live on and make a good life. The Lord has paid that price for you on the cross. He has paid for everything that I have done by his shedding blood.

I got a job at Tower home. I always got excited about a new job, thinking it would be good. I thought Tower would be different – new people. I thought the people wouldn't be so mean and nasty. I did meet a couple of people that were understanding. They had sympathy for me. They felt sorry for my life. They told me, 'Did you deserve better?' I was at Tower about three months. You didn't have to wear white uniforms there. The patients felt more at home there. The floors were different colors, so they know better where they were going. They were able to go downstairs some – they had good food.

I had more responsibility there. I enjoyed that because I never had the opportunity before. I thought, 'Wow – this is great.' I felt more important because I was able to do things that some of the nurses were doing, like taking blood pressures. I made pictures with the patients and wrote letters for them. We went to see some movies and stuff. We talked with them and had a kind of close relationship. That meant a lot to me. I don't recall what happened that I left. I wasn't doing something right on my job. Something went wrong.

After that is when I got the job as a chambermaid. That was my last job. There were so many Negroes at that job. It was about one-third white. There were twenty floors to do. We each had a floor with about seventeen or eighteen rooms. That meant from early morning until you finished you didn't get a break. It was like a half-hour break for lunch. If you stopped working you were dead. They would come around and check on you. They would check the dust with a white glove. I let that all go for a while, but then I said to myself, this isn't worth the money. You know, I was only getting about two dollars an hour – the vacuum cleaning and the scrubbing, the polishing. You had to make every little chrome thing in the bathroom shine. All those empty beer bottles and other stinking stuff – change the beds and make them. I felt they were going to use it the minute that you got out, so everything had to be in tip-top shape.

I could only get done about nine or ten rooms a day. I would never make it to my eighteen. I couldn't do it. They said I was slow and would send a girl down to help. That girl would boss me. She would tell me that the tub had a ring and go and do it. She would go out in the hall and smoke. I said, 'Forget it. I am not going to put up with this.' I was afraid to get on those elevators because of those colored people standing there and cussing and swearing. I told the lady that I couldn't do it any more. I had most of these jobs around the time I was staying with the Murdocks.

Everything was all right with the Murdocks, then she opened one of my letters from my mother. My mother and I were on bad terms and we were writing bad letters back and forth. We were swearing at each other in the letters. She opened up my letter and I came home and I said, 'Did I get any mail?' She said, 'Yeah. I opened it. It's from your mom.' That blew it right there. I got so upset. She told me that she didn't want me to get hurt. I used to sit down and talk to her about things, so she knew something was wrong with my mother and me. I told her, 'Don't open my letters.' I was ready to tear her head off. I told her she had no respect for me. Then her husband came home.

I would have liked to have stayed with the Murdocks but I got so carried away. My temper gets the best of me. I loved their baby. The husband said that we can't have Pattie 'cause she will hurt someone.

I don't know, I really believe that I have an emotional problem and I just can't control it when it happens. I have tried to stop myself. People would say, 'OK Pat, calm down,' but the more they talk the worse it gets. Little things start it, and then it builds up to a big huge dynamite thing.

I forget the name of the lady who came to get me. It was one of the attendants. I went back in a police car to the state school. I think this was in 1974.

Back to the Institution

They put me up in the hospital at the state school. The attendants didn't want me on the ward. They said that they didn't have a bed, but that wasn't true. I felt bad and cried. I always cry after something like that I am sorry I did it. I wouldn't eat and I wouldn't sleep. I just walked around my room.

When I came back to the state school they had moved into the new one. It had longer halls and nicer day rooms and furniture. It was much bigger. But the wards were smaller, twenty-four to a ward. We had a pantry where you could serve yourself. You didn't have to wait in line. They had a gym and a swimming pool. It still wasn't a good place to live – there were the same attendants – but the building was nice.

I stayed on the hospital ward a couple of weeks. Dr Newly came to see me a couple of times. He came to me and sat down on my bed and talked. He asked me why I get so emotional instead of calming myself down. I told him that I didn't think that I had any control over my emotional problems. I told him how it builds up and how my face gets red and I can't stop it. He was nice but he kept telling me that I needed medication, that my nerves were bad and I needed to be calmed down. He put me on medication and I stayed on it. All it did was dope me up. He told me that he wanted me to come and see him once a week after I got calmer. I went quite frequently to him. Even more than once a week.

All of a sudden, I just dropped coming to Dr Newly. He wasn't doing anything but taking down notes. He never even suggested anything. He would just write things down and that was it. I would sit there and wait for him to ask me questions. If he didn't, I just sat there because I wasn't going to volunteer any information. He asked me once why little kids bothered me. He asked me to look into my past. I told him about the other kids at my foster home and being thrown down the stairs. He said that that was an excuse to go on a rampage now. I told him that maybe it wasn't an excuse, but it was something people like him had to take into consideration.

He was the doctor I stole the records from. I just took them and didn't return them. I didn't like the stuff that was in them. A lot of it was lies. A lot of the things that they write up is not really the way it happened. It's the way they want to make it up to get you in trouble. They want you to stay longer. The more people they got in the school the more money they get. They put down there that I hit somebody with a stick and I never remember that. I remember kicking and turning over tables but I don't recall hitting anybody with anything. I might have but I don't remember it. When I get mad, it is a flash. I don't even realize what is happening.

The attendants talked about sex and the residents. Some of it was true. We are human. A lot of them did it right on the grounds. The girls came back and talked to me about it. The guys would come down and talk too. I was going with Noah Moody. He was a resident – a slick handsome guy, but he was stupid acting. He would do stupid things, like laugh and act dumb. He really wasn't that way, but because he was in that school he said to himself, 'They say I am stupid. I might as well act stupid – not show my intelligence.' He really had a lot on the ball. He showed me a lot of his school work. He was higher than I was. Everyone was treating him like a dumb-dumb: 'Come here. Do this. Be my flunky.'

I was going with him for at least a half year. When I came back I had a place above my old ward. They made me go up there and live because they didn't want me back down with the older kids – I was having too much trouble. That's when Noah and I started going together. It was a movie night – a Friday. We just saw each other and started talking. He said, 'I would like to know if you would like to go out with me.' I liked him OK. I liked him for everything he was. He had manners too. That guy wasn't dumb, not at all. If you snapped your fingers and told him to do something, he would do it. That's what the attendants used him for. He told me that he got beat up a lot of times from the men attendants. They beat up the guys a lot.

Me and Noah would see each other frequently. We would just sit down and talk. To me I felt I would like to get alone with him. I didn't go any further than kissing. I told him, 'Noah, you know I like you very much. I don't want to hurt you, but I don't think you were really meant for me.' I had this song 'It's Only Make Believe.' I had the record and I played it for him. I sat down and listened to it with him. I told him, 'You know that it is really only make believe. It is only make believe because we are in the state school. It might be real if we were on the outside. I would be able to go further with you.' So he says to me, 'Let's see, Pat. I don't really want to hurt you, I like you.' I didn't know what to say to him so we went our separate ways. He met another girl at school. She went a little further with him. He liked her, but he always came back to me. He always asked me to come to the side so he could talk to me.

When we were together, it was good. We walked hand in hand and went to the movies. He stole a couple of times. He came to me with a great big ring that looked like it could be a thousand dollars. He says, 'I bought this for you.' I said, 'Noah, I know darn well that you didn't buy that. You stole it, didn't you?' He looked at me with that little stupid grin. I said, 'I know all about it, Noah. I don't want it. Thank you anyways, but take it back.' He didn't take it back to where he got it. He gave it to his other girlfriend. She was stupid enough to take it.

One thing we had on the ward were period checks. In the old school there was this girl, I am not going to say any name, but she got pregnant after we started having those free times. They gave them for too long a time. Free time meant getting together with the boys with nobody around. We could go out walking with them. People started going down to the hot house – that's what we called it. It was like a fort that the guys made out of old logs and things that were laying around the grounds. It was like a hut. They used to put their coats down on the floor in it. I was going with Noah at the time. The attendants never told any of the girls about it – they never said a thing like, 'Look, this guy might do this and this guy might try that. You got to watch it.' They didn't tell them until one of the girls got knocked up. Then we were pushed into sex-education class. We had to go every day.

Girls started finding out about boys on their own. It was because the attendants weren't wise enough. They didn't really have what they thought they had in their heads – brains. This girl who it happened to, she was going with two or three different guys. They had her down to the fort. Not just here. They would say, 'Oh, come on down to the fort. I gotta show you what I built today.' They would run down the hill hand in hand. I asked, 'What's going on down there?' I walked by there once and Noah was in there. I said, 'What are you doing down here? You were supposed to pick me up. Noah,' I said, 'what are you doing down here?' He said, 'Come on in.' I said, 'No. I'm not going in there. I know what's going on.' He said, 'What?' 'I know you guys are getting those girls. That is not right. You are using them.' He said, 'We are going to use you some day when you find out all about it.' I said, 'No, you're not either, because I am smart enough to understand. I am not stupid like some of the girls.' Some of the guys got caught down there in that fort. They had to go to STA – Special Treatment Area – for males. It was really lockup.

A lot of the troublemakers were Spanish guys from New York City. They called themselves a gang. Those tough ones thought they could run the world and everything. New York City black, Spanish, white, whatever they were, they were trouble. Like I said, one of the girls got knocked up from one. She should have known better – no one told her.

Other girls got pregnant too. They were took right up to the hospital. They had to go up there and they called the doctor. One girl was pregnant and she had to get an abortion. No one was supposed to have a baby at the school.

With the fort, some girls wanted it and some didn't. The girls that were walking around and the guy would just run out and say come on. They would squirm and start screaming. I would call that rape. If she say no and the guy says yes, that is rape, as far as I am concerned.

Some of the girls enjoyed talking about what was going on with the boys. They didn't talk too much around the wards about the hanky-panky, because the attendants sat right in back at the table. Some of them would be talking about it. 'This girl is this and they got that one knocked up.' The attendants shouldn't be gossiping. As far as I am concerned it would destroy me if someone was saying that about me.

They would write everybody's names down and they would check to see if you had a period. They would mark it for that month. If you missed a couple of months they would send you up to the doctor right away. They would force you to show your period – that was some of the stuff that they did that was really cruel.

Out Again

After I stayed at the new state school a while, I kept bugging them to get me out. My friend, John, arranged for me to go live with this family up at the university. He was a professor and she was too. I liked it. I was on the third floor – it was cozy. I had my own bath and I could get away. I had my own room. I like Annie – the wife – she was considerate of me. I loved the children. They were much different than any other children I have ever met. I don't know if it was their education from the professional family or what, but they were different. They were so much more intelligent and had so much more respect and they could do things that kids their age just couldn't. They knew so much about other countries and weaving and stuff, it was fascinating.

Just the whole setting was peaceful. It wasn't nerve-wrecking. No one ever hollered at me. I was always volunteering to do something. I was willing to do anything. I liked the five-year-old. He was cute. It was just a peaceful atmosphere. There was just a whole different atmosphere there – no-pressure home. No one demanded anything. It was a whole different way of life. If the atmosphere you live in is calm then you are going to be calm.

While I was living there something happened with me and a volunteer from the school. She was supposed to be my friend – you know, help me out. Her name was Lucy. She was my friend until she called me retarded once. She said, 'You are retarded. That is why you can't do some things like school work.' She was really upset with me because I had gotten upset myself. She told me that she would be home to take care of her little girl – I was watching her. I wanted to catch the last bus because I had no other way home. She said that she would be home in time. I really got mad. I said, 'You know this isn't right, Lucy. You said to take care of your girl until a certain time. I'm not babysitting anymore.' I was crying and upset, but I didn't do anything but stand there and hollering. Then she started hollering and told me that she didn't want me to come to her house no more. Then she said that about me being retarded and then we got into it good. I took a cab back to the house at the university and had to borrow the money to pay.

Then I had to leave the university place. The people at the school made me go – I thought it was wrong. I couldn't stay because my room was on the third floor and that's against state regulations. They couldn't think about my happiness, only about their regulations.

After I had to leave there – I was there six weeks – I went over to the Kings. That Mrs King was a big mother. I wasn't sure about moving there. When I first saw her I said to myself that this woman is going to use me and the state school for the money. She was talking about money all the time – how she didn't have money for this and didn't have money for that. She got money from the state for having me and another girl there. Some of it was for clothes, but we never saw that. The house – the Kings' – wasn't very nice on the outside, but I had a big bedroom all to myself. The place was in a very bad section of the city. It was on the west side. You couldn't go out of the house at night. There were fights and arguments in the street and everything. It wasn't a good atmosphere for anyone. It was only a few blocks from the state school. She had this guy that was living with her. He would sleep with her, but there were times when he wouldn't come in at all. His name was Roy. He was nice but he had a bad attitude. He didn't sit down and talk with anybody. There were two other girls besides me. Mrs King was getting paid $300 a month for each of us.

I met my boyfriend of that time downtown. I was standing by a window looking at something – a pants suit or a dress or something. I always loved clothes. I saw him and he saw me and our eyes connected with each other. I started to walk into the store and he came behind and opened the door for me. That started it right there. He asked me if I would like to go down and have coffee with him. So we went down to a coffee shop and had something to drink and left. He asked me if I would like to go and meet his mother. That day I had supper with them.

I used to like to go downtown and look around – walk around and look at the clothes. That's the way I met all of my friends. I am pretty popular with the guys. They just start talking to me – they like me. A lot of people get the wrong impression. I didn't have friendly visits with everyone I met. People might think that the first night with them that is it – that is not true at all. It is just with people that I think that I care a lot for – someone that I think is going to care for me. I just want to show my love.

Mrs King was nice at times. We went to church a lot. I liked the church at first and then I didn't because it just didn't mean as much to me – not as much as my own. Everybody was colored in there – nobody was white. Not the sight of one white person there. I felt out of place. I stopped going and she said what was the matter with me. I told her that I just don't feel like going. She wanted to know what was wrong. One night she went and I went out with this guy and I didn't come home that night at all. She was really mad. She asked me why I didn't tell her. I went back to get a pair of flats to wear that morning. I wasn't really coming back. She started yelling, 'Why aren't you coming home?' I said I was going out and I would talk to her later. I decided to move out. Roy locked me out. I said the hell with it.

I wasn't at the Kings' a month. The atmosphere was something else. There were beer joints and people hollering and screaming. Loud music. You should have heard it coming from Marsh Street – one night the music was so loud you could hear it for four blocks. I didn't think that was right.

I found my own apartment and really moved out. I was working at St Matthew's Hospital. I made enough money the first two weeks and said the heck with it. I felt good. This was a big stepping stone in my life. I never had an apartment and that was fantastic to me. The apartment I got was just a few blocks from there. All those beer joints and whore houses – the Red Inn, that was a whore house. All kinds of things went on in there. Everything you could think of. The guy I was going with wanted me to go there. I went in there and there was these girls and these guys – they were doing it right there on the floor – they didn't care. It was a drinking place on the outside, but they were whoring it right there. He was telling me that it wasn't a whore place – it was just what people did when they got high. When I get high I don't do it in front of everybody. I was shocked – now they have changed the place and it's different.

When I was working at St Matthew's, I set up trays and things. I spilled scalding hot coffee all over me and they had to rush me to the emergency room. They ice-packed me, because I was

burned. I don't have no scars or anything. I only got two checks
from St Matthew's and then they fired me.

After I moved to my own place I just decided that it was all over. I dated a lot of guys during that time – I would say about seven. That was just in one month. I just went to this bar. The guys were just pushing the money – 'Give that girl a drink down here' – you know, that kind of stuff. I figured that they paid for my drinks I felt that I owed them something. Not every time that I left with one of them did I have sex, but if I liked that person it was that night. It was one of those things.

I was going to start living it up. I went out to parties till 3:00 and 4:00 in the morning – came home drunk. I felt I couldn't do it any other time. I couldn't do it living with families because it would be a problem. I felt that I am human and I am young and I need my desires just like anybody else. A lot of people say that they didn't have it until they were married. Don't give me that line of baloney. They would say, 'Oh, Pattie, you are a nice young girl and shouldn't do this. You should wait until you get married and find the right guy.' Happier people are the people that get to know their man before they get married. If you like them, you know. If you just clam up with someone and if you are not satisfied with what they have to offer, well then you are not going to be happy. You are going to have a divorce and have to go through all that garbage. There is just no sense in it. That is the story of my life.

I didn't feel strange about it. That is the way that I was cut out. I wasn't able to get together with anybody before, because I was always tied up with other people. I felt free and open. I loved it. It was my character to like sex. They liked me – I know that they did. They liked the way I treated them – the way that I satisfied people.

The first time I went to a bar I felt a little strange. I didn't know exactly what was going to happen. My girlfriends told me that there was nothing wrong in it. I didn't listen to anybody that said that you can get hurt when you go into a bar.

After I lost my job, I met this guy, Harry Blass. He was always dating somebody else – or with someone when he was supposed to be with me. He had a car and a job working on a truck. He lived next door to me. I met him when he was sitting on his porch. I was out on my porch talking with my girlfriend from upstairs. I went inside and brought out something to drink. I was drinking heavily then – beer and wine and whiskey with gingerale. I said to my girlfriend, 'Why don't you go up to him and see if he is dating?' I wanted him so bad it wasn't even funny. She went and asked him and found that he wasn't dating. I said, 'Great. Go back and ask him if I could have a date with him.' So he came over to my house and knocked on the door. I said, 'Hello.' He said that he was Harry. I opened the door and he came and sat down on the couch. He said, 'I heard you wanted a date. Why didn't you ask? I would be more than welcome. You are a pretty girl.' That went to my head.

We went riding around in his car and we started talking and we kissed. The second month we started getting into it. He had the apartment right in back of me and we had a door between us and we opened it and were going in and out of each other's apartment. He would live with me and I would live with him. He paid my rent, because I lost my job. He didn't want me to go. That's why he paid it. He made good money.

Our relationship stopped because I met the Spanish guy. Harry went out with this other girl. He didn't think I saw him, but I saw when he was turning the corner. When he came home I was so mad. I told him that I had seen the girl. I told him that I had been going out, too, since I thought he was. I told him I was dating a Spanish guy. I told him that he better get out of my life.

I started going out with a lot of Spanish guys. The Spanish guys are pretty cool. They had their own place – their own little shack that they built. They would go there if they didn't have any other place to go.

I liked all the bars – except the Mexican one. They were mean. I don't know if it was Mexican. They were a little darker than

Puerto Ricans so I thought it was Mexican. When they got drunk
they were very wild. I am kind of scared of them.

The boyfriends in Central City never worked out. I kind of overdid it. I used to go to the bars and they used to sit there and we used to drink a lot. I can handle myself a lot better. I used to go to the High Life, Tony's, and Murphy's down there on Main Street. I went to the Spanish bar across from it and over the north side at the People's Grill. I used to go to parties at night until 2:00 in the morning. I don't do that now. I smoked marijuana. I don't do that kind of stuff now.

I'm embarrassed about my boyfriends in Central City. Smoking marijuana and doing things you are not supposed to do until you get married and stuff – that is just an old tradition. You know that you are not supposed to do this and you're not supposed to do that. The church believes you save yourself for a married man. It is so hard at times, though. I am a woman. We are all human. We have the times when we are more sensitive than others. Things happen that wouldn't happen at another time. That's what happened in Central City. But I don't care for it right now, because that's not all there is to life – just having fun and having a baby – caring for it the rest of your life and all that responsibility.

Well, anyway, I lost my apartment 'cause I couldn't pay the rent. I got evicted. Then I went to live with my mother and then my sisters.

Boy, I ended my stay with my sister good. My sister called me retarded too. We were mad. I was living in the trailer with her and her husband. It was last September. Before this time we got along pretty good. Mom and I never got along. I was staying with my mom and got into a big argument. I started asking, 'Why was I in that school? How come you had to put me there? Why did you dislike me all my life? Why couldn't it have been a happier life? Why couldn't you and dad get back together? Why can't we have all our family together?' She said, 'It is not going to happen, honey, so you might as well stop dreaming about that kind of stuff.' It made me upset, so I told her I would like to leave. I said I wanted to go and live with my sister. She came down and said, 'Sure, Pat. We will take Pat.' That was a wrong move to begin with. Her husband was my boyfriend at one time. He met her through me and that is when they started dating. I felt very upset about it – very jealous whenever I see him with her. It was the wrong step to ever bring me into her home with her husband.

She went grocery shopping a lot and left me home. I didn't like that. I like to go shopping and riding instead of staying home cleaning the house. We were getting along for about two months, then all of a sudden, bang, everything started happening. We started fighting about why dad did this and why mom did that. One day she took me down to my father's place in Brookville. He lives in a trailer park.

Everything was fine when we were with him, but once we got back in the car she said, 'Why didn't you start yourself in front of dad?' One thing is that my father loves me better than her. She did some real bad things when he had her on vacation. She broke his furniture and a lot of stuff that was precious to him. This is when she got mad. She swore at him. I break furniture too, but not at dad and mom's house. Dad said that she wasn't even worthy of trying to help because she wasn't going to better herself. When we were at his place he looked over to me and said, 'Pat has really come a long way.' He was actually proud of me more than her. She would dress like a tomboy. I always wore dresses. I never had jeans. I never owned a pair in my life.

When we got in the car, she said why didn't I start something in front of dad because she thought she would start talking about the letter. I wrote a bad letter to him one time because he got on my nerves. He came home drinking and I asked him why we couldn't go out riding with the whole family some time. He was drunk, and you don't talk about anything when he is drunk. You got to leave him by himself and he gets over it. I should have known better. He grabbed me and threw me. I hit him and that ended it. But he beat me first. Then I wrote him this letter. I told

him what a bad guy he was and that he should stop drinking
and be a better father to the kids. I did put a couple of cussing
words in there. See, he was expecting miracles out of us and yet
he wasn't expecting anything for himself. My sister read the letter, but it wasn't any of her business. In the car, she said, 'You
were so sweet and innocent in front of him after you wrote that
nasty letter.' She wrote my mother once and told her she was a
whore – so she shouldn't talk. It hurt my mother's feelings too.

In the car we got into a big argument. I started to cry and
scream at her. She got nervous. I told her that I wish she would
die. She said, 'I want you out of this car. You can walk home.' I
said, 'I am not walking from here.' She pulled over to push me
out. I said, 'Martha, we have both had a rough life.' I tried to
soften her. I do that when people are really upset with me. I told
her, 'We shouldn't get so angry with each other. Try to think
about it and talk about it instead of getting upset.' That didn't
work. She got more upset about different things. She told me
that my mother couldn't stand me. Right there and then I hit her
and pulled her hair. Good thing that car was stopped because we
would have been in a good accident. We were like lions ripping
each other apart.

When we got home she said she was going to call the police. I
tried to soften her up because all the neighbors would know
about it. When we got home she didn't even pick up the phone
but she got inside the door and pulled a knife out. I kicked her
and took it out of her hand. I took her down on the ground. I
punched her. She is bigger than I am. I mean big, I mean fat, too.
I punched her in the face, bit her on the neck, pulled her hair;
she had beautiful long hair. She pulled mine. She ripped my
blouse. I ripped hers. We were going at each other like wild animals. Finally the police came. I don't know who called them,
probably the neighbors, 'cause there was hollering and screaming. She picked up the drain board and threw it and I threw it
right back.

I broke her collarbone and she broke this finger. It is OK now, but the bone was way out here. The doctor had to put it back. I called my mom and told her that I wanted to come home. She said, 'What's wrong, what's wrong?' I said, 'My sister and I had a fight.' I was crying. She said, 'I am not coming to get you.' Right away fighting was out. She don't like to hear about us getting in trouble like that. If my brother-in-law came home he would of killed me she told me that. He was working at Maximum Steel down on the west side.

You see, when we started the fight she called me retarded. She said the reason you have been in all those state schools is because you are retarded – 'You are stupid looking.'

I had no place to go. I didn't want to go back to the state school, so I called John. The police took me to the hospital for my finger. Just me – she went later with my brother-in-law. After we got back on good terms she told me that my brother-in-law told her that he didn't want to see me around the trailer or he would kill me.

When the police came they broke us up. I was happy to see them. He said, 'Who belongs here, anyway?' My sister told them that she did and that I didn't belong. She didn't tell them how she wanted me there at first. She told them that I came because I had to come.

My sister stole some of the clothes that I left there. She packed things when I wasn't there and left some of my stuff out. I didn't see my brother-in-law after that. Good thing, because when Puerto Ricans get mad, boy, watch out. He took her to Oregon and that's where they are now. She is pregnant. She couldn't get pregnant for four years. She had her tubes blown open by a machine. They were putting her on fertilizer pills. They didn't do any good and then, finally, she got pregnant.

There is this guy that lives here in Woodard. He used to live right next to them out in the trailer park. They smoked marijuana together. He told me about them moving and her being pregnant. I am glad for her. Her not having a baby kind of threw them apart for awhile.

The police took me to the emergency room and I was crying all
the way because of the pain. After I didn't have my mother to
come to they came back and drove me to the county line and the
state school picked me up and took me to John's door.

I stayed there about a week and then I found a family to live
with out in Melrose which is right near Woodard. Woodard is
about forty miles from Central City. I watched the kids, but that
didn't work out either. That's when I moved here. It's a small
town but it's OK – especially the people and the religion.

Present Life

I am on my own. Right now I make $2.10 an hour. That's $132
every two weeks as my net pay. After they take the tax out and I
bring it home it's about $112. This last check, I got $100 because I
missed some days, so I wasn't able to pay my landlord the full
amount due. I told him that I would give him his $50 now, and I
would give him his $30 plus $70 when I get paid again. The rent
is $150 so I pay him $70 one time and $80 the other.

I went to the welfare department to try to get some extra
money and they said, 'We can't help you. You make enough
money.' I can't see where I make enough money. I need the help.
Like there is no food in the house sometimes. They told me that
that was too bad.

Meat is expensive and fish isn't cheap. I buy frozen vegetables
because I like them better than the canned stuff. You don't know
what's in those cans. I used to have ice cream and stuff like that,
but I don't have sweets now.

I don't have a lot of clothes. I had to give a lot of them away
because they were too big. My skirts are falling off around my
hips and stuff. That's what's bad about a diet – especially if you
don't have much money.

I am on a diet. I'm down to 168. The doctor gave me a two-
weeks' supply of medication and diet pills. He's on vacation –
comes back the twenty-eighth. I will be going back to see him.

When I left the Cornerstone State School, I was 189. I did not go up or down when I was in the state school. I was very emotionally upset most of the time. Things were happening and I was acting up and doing something stupid.

This is the least I have weighed since I got out. That is because it is a nice peaceful atmosphere here. Nobody bothers you. There is no one here when I get upset or depressed. I just let it go. It gets off. When I am with people and I know that I am depressed somebody starts bugging me – saying, 'What's wrong?' It makes me worse. That is one good thing about living by yourself. You are able to get over it quickly.

The major problem with people leaving the state school is that you are so used to everything being handed to you. Like your food is provided, and you don't have to cook. You don't know how to do your laundry. They do it for you. They won't let you touch the washer. When you get out, it is no fun because you don't know what the outside is all about. They don't tell you about expenses, like food. I never learned anything about food. I never had to get a balanced meal before getting out. They never showed you what a nutritional diet was. They never showed you that. When you get out you're lost. You gotta go 'round asking people and you feel kind of stupid. Here you are in an apartment. If you are in an apartment, people would look at you and think you don't know what you are doing. You ask these questions that everybody else knows. It gets them wondering.

They didn't show me how to buy clothes, either. They didn't tell you about comparing prices. I would go out and buy clothes for $20 that I could get for $15.

Mrs Mack, my friend from the church I belong to, took me food shopping last Saturday. She is the lady that I am going to live with. It is a nice family. She said to me, 'Pat, let me take you shopping and I will help you compare prices.' So she took me to the store. Let me tell you, going with her and learning how to compare prices and how to find out what's the best buy helped

me save. I usually come home with only two bags and I came
home with three and still had extra money in my pocket to
spend. This is because she took me. When I go by myself I
picked up anything. I don't really stop to think what I'm buying.
I'm in a big hurry, in such a rush. Somebody is behind you
pushing you along and you grab anything.

When you get out of the state school you don't know where to
go. You don't know where to turn to, and if you don't find
friends you are just stuck. I can't speak for everybody, everybody
has their own way. But people coming out either turn the person
off that is helping them or they turn them on. I am speaking for
myself now, but I feel I have been successful outside because I
have listened to people with advice. If someone would say, 'OK
now, Pat, why don't you go to the store and try it?' I would.

My pastor helped me to budget. He showed me the different
things about budgeting. Church has always been something for
me, because I found people who were really able and willing to
help. In Central City they weren't as friendly as they are here,
but I had gotten some good advice there, too – not about food
and clothing but about different things. But you know this
church has really helped me with budgeting.

I would say I know about fifteen people who have left the state
school. There was a girl living next to me and there was a girl
that left and went home with her mom. There was another one
that went with her mother, and then there was two or three that
went to East Chester with their family. These were on the ward
with me.

There are other people you see walking around. Mary Jo is by
herself. She is getting married. She is about twenty-five – not
really old. She has her problems. I guess she is getting married
because she has to. That's not good, either. I see her and Norine
and Sally. Norine Edwards used to be on the old ward at Cornerstone way back. She lives on her own in an apartment. She shops
for herself and takes care of the apartment. It's a beautiful little

efficiency apartment and she keeps it well cleaned. She doesn't work right now. She's on social security and her father sent her $5,000. I don't know what it was for, but she told me that. She's got things and knows what she is doing. She's here in town. A nervous type. If she don't have a person with her that she knows, she won't do anything. I asked her to come to church with me just to try to see if she liked it, but she would have to come with me.

The other night, at the night school I go to, I had a talk with the principal about retardation. I said to him, 'Why do you call them kids retarded?' He said, 'Because they are not normal like we are. They are not able to do the things that we can. They need an awful lot of help which we don't.' I said, 'Do you really think that they should be called retarded? Why can't they be called people that need help?' He said, 'Well, because retarded is the word for that.' That really made me mad, so I just got up and took off – waited for my ride and then went.

In Empire we had religious training but it wasn't the religion I know now. We didn't do anything – it wasn't moving, it wasn't meaningful, as it is now. You did a lot of singing. Just singing and sitting down and then singing again. We got up and recited prayers.

The church I go to now is having a banquet party, Friday. It is going to be for us, the Bible School. It is going to be for graduation. We are going to get our certificates. It means that we went through the course. There will be fifty or sixty people from the church. It will be a covered-dish supper and a graduation cake. Each person is going to make something and come with their dish. I am on the committee. Mom – Mrs Mack – is, too. She goes around and gets people to make things. I am bringing celery sticks and carrots and little odds and ends.

Religion is all over me. It means something; it means my life. They call it the Pentecost movement. The Bible talks about it. All the prophets and the apostles and Jesus got together in the upper room for the Last Supper. There was a break-out, speaking in tongues – in each person's own language. They started talking to the Lord in his tongues. This is His gift to us. When you cry or you ask Him for the gift, He gives it to you. This is what the Pentecost movement is. It is experiencing a lot of things. It is experiencing the speaking of tongues. If you can speak in tongues you also can interpret it. The interpreter gives the message to the believers.

It is different from the first church I went to – the one that I met the Bakers at – the Assembly church on Barr Street. The first thing that drew me close to that church was the people – their friendliness, their warmth, their consideration, their love. It was so strong that I thought that there gotta be something in it. Then I received Jesus Christ into my life. I received Him in August in 1974.

The way of inviting the Lord into your heart is just plain hearing the Word, hearing the Word is revealed in your mind. Then after you hear the Word you start saying, 'Wow, this is gotta be real. Why would that pastor stand up there all that time and start talking about stuff like that if it wasn't real? Why would he waste his time just talking there?' The Bible is real, it has gotta be. That is when I just realized that it is the real thing. I said, 'Pattie, you need that in your life. This will straighten you out.' It has helped me a lot.

When Jesus Christ came into my life everything was different. I didn't have to cry over my problems. I didn't have to worry about them. It says in the Bible that the Lord loves us so much that He sent His only son to die for us. I figured if this is true, the Lord will show me something. Once we receive Him we are His child and there is a spiritual birth. In a lot of churches you will never hear this. There is a spiritual birth. It is not going back to your mom's womb a second time. It is being spiritually born again. It is from heaven – from the Lord Jesus Christ Himself who died on the cross for us. It is just accepting the Lord Jesus Christ as your personal savior and then letting Him go and fill you with His holy spirit.

I really didn't find anything interesting in religion before. I would go to church but I didn't get anything out of it. When I went I just played with the books and things – I didn't care.

God knows everything. He knows the heart, He knows the mind. He knows what we are doing. A lot of people think after they are saved and you do wrong – like a little incident like me and Josh – that the Lord casts you off. That's not true. All of that dying on the cross and shedding of blood for us wouldn't have been worth it if that were true.

The Bakers were in the first church I was in. I sat by them one or two times. They saw that I was being sincere. A lot of people can tell you by your attitude and actions. You change and it is not like someone putting on a show saying, 'OK, Lord, here I am.' It doesn't make you popular, taking the Lord. I have lost an awful lot of friends because I came to Jesus. People wouldn't believe me that I took the Lord. I have shown them the Bible and I have shown them the different passages and messages but they still won't believe me. I have been praying for them. I have got a few people saved already. They accepted Jesus Christ.

I have been in this religion, Pentecostal, for a long time. I am really happy with it. I made a lot of good friends. I always have people that I can talk to. There is people that will help in time of need. It's hard to find that in this world. Everybody is busy – just too busy to help. They care. Mrs Mack has brought me things over – a lamp stand and a tray. She has brought me different things for my apartment. I figure if people care, I should care.

The other day, the lady I am going to be staying with, Mrs Mack, got on one of the subjects that I don't care to talk about, at least not then. I told her to just leave me alone. I got sensitive to it. I started talking right back to her – kind of started a little argument. One of the friends was sitting in the back seat and she said, 'Pat, don't be so sensitive.' That is hard, you know? It's just how you take what people say. I said, 'I won't tell you why I am sensitive, but there is some stuff deep inside that it's about.'

What Mrs Mack was talking about was how I had such a poor life. People saying that stuff about me having a poor life sounded sympathetic when you want to hear it, but not all the time. Sometimes I just don't want to be pitied. Why should people say, 'You poor child. You have had a rough life?' I know that I have had a rough life. Why should they make it so grim? Everything has changed. It is better now. Why should people pity me by looking at things that happened a long time ago? I would rather they said, 'Well, look at this girl. She is really great. She has come a long way. She is not a poor child. She is learning, she is doing that and that.' I would rather hear that than, 'That poor life you had to know.' I don't care about that life. That was way back when. It is all taken care of. I am not thinking about it. I am in this world now and I gotta make it now. People saying, 'Oh, you poor child,' soon I am going to hear that too much. I am just trying to show them that I am not a poor child. I want them to see what this grand child is doing for herself. The poor child stuff just doesn't turn me on now. Before I was looking for pity because I felt sorry for myself. I have grown up about it. I have realized that things have happened that I can't change.

A lot of people are sensitive to things that have happened to people in their past. For instance, Mrs Mack is very sensitive to what she has heard about my past. I felt she needed to know because I will be living with her and she has got to understand.

There was this incident when I went to stay with her for a weekend. She said something like, 'Pat, why do you get so sensitive when people say certain things? Why do you take it so serious? Why can't you just forget it?' I told her, 'I have been hurt too much. I am just going to let you know a little bit about what happened to me because I am going to be living with you.' So I told her some things about the school and my early life. She said, 'Pat, I am glad that you told me. Now I know why you are so sensitive.' Now she isn't bugging me as much in sensitive areas. She knows when to stop. I have done the same for her. I know when not to talk to her and when to. I know when she will like something and when she doesn't. I guess that you just have to learn that with people. It is learning every day of your life, it just doesn't stop.

The attendants weren't like that at all. They all thought that all they had to do is make these kids mind. They were going to do it by punishing us and acting high over us. This is the way I see it, not the way they said it. I think that is why I reacted a lot to the things that they did. I had very strong opinions and we weren't able to express ourselves the way that we would like to.

I really don't want to go and live with the Macks. I want to live by myself. When I get upset I am here alone and there is no audience around. I am able to get over it. I feel it coming and I know how to get over it. I say to myself, 'Pat, let's go and listen to the radio.' I do want to go and live with them because it would be someone to talk with. I would be able to make more friends. Now I am here all the time and I can't get out because I have no car. She's got a car. She says she will introduce me to some friends that I could go out with. No drinking or anything – just being together. I don't drink anyways – not now. I would have my own room, but when I live around other kids I get frustrated inside – jealous.

If I moved I just feel that I will be part of a family. I will do the things that they do. I can help out. They like me and I like them. We can talk about things – things that are bothering us. We let it out in the open. She does, too. It is just becoming a habit now. I do it all the time.

She said she doesn't mind me calling her mom. She said that it doesn't bother her. She has got so many daughters in the Lord anyways. They might as well have another one. That makes me feel good. She said she wouldn't expect me to call her anything else.

I already ordered her Christmas present through Sears. I will get it at the end of the week. I got her a long, bright-red gown with a hood. She likes that style with a slit up the side. I got her son some wheat-colored jeans and some shaving stuff. He doesn't

shave but he uses it – oh, he likes the smell of it. I got her
daughter a sleeping bag and pajamas.

I think I will get married. I definitely want to get married right
now, but I don't have anybody to get married to. I expressed that
to Joshua and I haven't really known him that long. I shouldn't
have done that. I probably will scare him away.

I met Joshua through Honey Marshall. She's got her own
apartment. She lives upstairs and he lives downstairs. She called
him up when I was at her place. She told him that she got someone that wants to be introduced. This was just this Friday night.
I was visiting her. She told him to come up. Joshua knocks on the
door and comes in. His eyes almost popped out. I said, 'Hi
Joshua,' and he said, 'Hi.' I went over and sat on the couch and
we started talking. It was interesting. There was no one else in
the room except me. Honey used to be at Cornerstone State
School but her friend Marlene from down the hall wasn't.

It was kind of strange the way Joshua was looking at me. He
said that I should come out in the hall because he wanted to talk
to me. I went and we talked. He told me, he says, 'Do you think
that I can show you someone that really cares and likes you?' I
had told him a little, not a lot, just enough to hit him, about
myself. I told him that my life has been no pleasure. He says that
you really had a rough life, and said, 'Well, honey, maybe someone needs to show you what a good life is.'

We started going out, and he took me to the movies the other
night. Our pastor was kind of upset, though, because I didn't go
to Bible School. He came over here and we watched TV that first
night. He works in the steel mill on Center Street. He picks up
this heavy steel and has to put it in the heat. He has a hard job
and he gets like $6 an hour. He says he brings home a good
chunk. He is not worried. He has a good car – a brand-new car
and everything. He is twenty-nine years old – nine years older
than I am. I am glad. I would rather have my man older. It don't
look good the other way.

He is from Philadelphia. He couldn't get a job there, so he came here and he has been working since. He will stay here until he changes his mind. He graduated and he is a smart guy. He said that if I need any help in arithmetic or school work he could help me.

Joshua doesn't want me to go to church. I told him that this Sunday I could come and visit him, but after church. He doesn't believe in ministers. He doesn't believe in this and that. I am too attached to my church right now. I'm not going to worry about it. If he doesn't like it, too bad.

When Josh came from Philadelphia he was in – I don't know if I should say this – I am going to, I don't care what people think, either. He was put in prison because he did robbery. He told me that. He said, 'I want you to know that from the beginning, so that you understand.' I said, 'Josh, that doesn't matter to me what you did in your life back then. It is what happens right now.' He said, 'I am glad that you think that way, because a lot of people would forget about me when they hear that I was in prison.' I said, 'Josh, if I really wanted you and need you, I wouldn't do that. I really need you. I would like to see you a lot.'

I wouldn't tell Josh that I was at the state school. I don't have any explanation to tell him. Maybe later, but right now it is too much for him to take. Later, if we did get a relationship really strong, I would tell him. Sometimes your mouth slips. You might be saying something and you don't realize because you are not listening. I wouldn't tell him about the straitjackets or about how wicked and mean I was. He doesn't really have to know that.

I would like to have a little girl. You can dress them up in little bonnets and little bows and stuff like that. When it started getting hot and heavy, Josh told me that if I had a child it would be my doings. He is afraid of the support and knowing that I am going to be happy after I have it.

I have always wanted a baby that I can call my own. There is a social worker up in Woodard that said to me, 'Pat, it is not just having a child and loving it, it is taking care of it, providing for it. They don't stay little forever. The bigger they get, the bigger the problems. You have to stop and think about that.' I have thought about that.

I want to have children so that I can make a life for them. I have to give myself more credit for myself than she does. I can take care of a child. I have babysat. She said, 'That's different. Being with them twenty-four hours a day is different.' I told her, 'I'm able.' I know how to make a formula and change diapers. In fact, when I was babysitting I would almost make the child mine. I did because I want one so bad. I talked to Josh about it. Josh doesn't think it is a good idea. He is afraid that I won't be able to support it. Right now I have financial problems.

He is living with another woman that he is supporting. He is paying everything for her while she goes to school. She doesn't want to work. I am working and going to school and he thinks that is great because I am helping myself. He told me the other day, 'Pat, I like you, you are a nice girl, but you know I have financial problems. Right now I am trying to take care of this woman.' I have been tempted to tell him that I don't want to be an in-betweener. I feel sometimes that I am being used. I haven't been able to tell him that, though. I have just been clammed up about that.

Things really got hot and heavy when he was here. I will put it bluntly. We did have intercourse. It has been a long time and I just need my needs and satisfaction and he needed his. I said to myself, 'This isn't good.' I told him right from the beginning, before we even made bodily contact, that it isn't right. I said, 'You disrespect me now and treat me just like any person.' He said, 'Pat, don't compare me with other people you have known. If I say that I will be coming back, I will.' He said, 'Don't worry about what the church has taught you. You are not going to hell.'

I know that I am not going to hell for it. I don't think you should have sex outside of marriage, but it has happened so many times that I don't feel guilty about it anymore, but I told him, 'You are going to lose your respect for me.' I wouldn't be telling you this, but he went on and on. I told him that I don't want him to leave. He told me that he didn't want me to move in with a family. I said I don't want to either. That is how close I felt to him at the time. I still do. Before I went to Central City last week he called me three times telling me that he didn't want me doing anything foolish in Central like fooling around with anybody. I know he cared or he wouldn't have said that about Central to me.

I said that he must care for that girl more than he cares for me or else he would move in with me and leave her. Now that I am talking about it, it is making me think that it is either me or her – he has to make a choice. Even though he met my needs, I will feel guilty if he leaves. I mean bang, bang, and it will be over, but that is the way it will have to be. It has been almost a year.

He told me that he would come over the next night and I waited for him until about 10:00. I fell asleep and I got up about midnight. I started thinking, 'This guy has used me. He has gone and forgotten about me.' It really was bothering me. The next day he called me up at work and said, 'Honey, where were you last night?' I said, 'What do you mean where was I? I was on the couch sleeping and waiting for you.' He said, 'I thought you might be doing something with somebody else.' That ticked me off. He said that he came. I told him that he was full of it. He said that he could prove it because he said that your keys were in the door. They were too. I told him that I was sorry and that he did come that night. I had to apologize because it was my mistake.

He told me that he would like to see me before I left, but he didn't. I called him at work. He told me to watch myself and not to do anything foolish in Central City. I said, 'OK, you do the same.' That was a joke, because I know I can't stop him when he is with his women. He said, 'Can I see you on Friday night when you come back?' I told him that I had a meeting. He told me to cancel that business stuff. I told him that I was going and that he would have to hang loose for a while. He said, 'You don't love me.' I told him that if I didn't I wouldn't have anything to do with him.

It doesn't look like he is going to be a permanent thing. I am not going to worry about it. In fact, I am not putting myself in a position where if he does leave me that I am going to break to pieces. He is just there for my needs. That's all that I care about right now.

I have to put some heavy thought on it. If Joshua doesn't come tonight and doesn't come tomorrow night, then I feel that he has made up his mind. He is not going to go with a churchgoer and that's all there is to it, or he doesn't care.

If I get pregnant I am not going to worry about it. I will take that when it comes. That's right, let's take it when it comes. Me worried about it? Not me. The people at welfare wouldn't look down on me or anything, but they would say, 'Pat, we have tried to teach you better than that. Why did you have to be so foolish?' They are so kind, and then they are not. I have experienced so many times that they say something nice and then say something else that really makes me feel so hurt. If I do it, it's my problem not theirs. No one is taking it away from me, that's for sure. There is no problem there. I am not going to let it happen. I don't think I'm pregnant now. I am in my safety period right now. You know, five days before your period, you usually don't ovulate any more. I am not worried about it. If it happens, it happens. I will start worrying about it when I see something popping up.

I was on birth-control pills, but I got off them because they were making me fat and bloated and my heart was beating too fast. I was throwing up and wasn't feeling too good in the morning. I thought that I was pregnant but I wasn't, it was just the pill. The doctor said that I can't take them. He tried to give me the loop and I wouldn't take that either. They hurt. A lot of people get pains from them and they bleed more. I couldn't take it. I am already bleeding nine days as it is. I couldn't take more. Forget it. It's bad enough that I have to spend all that money for Tampax.

I started with the pills when I was messing around a lot in Central City. When I was going out to bars and dating and I had my own apartment.

I do and don't think you should do it before you're married. I kind of believe you shouldn't before, but I figured there is no sense in thinking that way when it is already broke. Whatever I think now, it has already happened and so how can you think about it that way? It happened before anybody ever really gave me good advice or talked to me. How in the world can you say that that is the way it should be? Well, that's the way I feel now. There is no way that I could save myself for my husband.

So I don't feel bad, but, like, if I went to the pastor or some of the families in the church and told them, they would look down on me so fast that it wouldn't be funny. If I came in that church pregnant they wouldn't throw me out, but they wouldn't be as warm and as friendly as they are right now. They would be very disappointed, let's put it that way. They think that I am the best girl, the sweetest and kindest and all that kind of stuff. I am sweet, but I have my ways of doing it. The family that I am going to live with knows I've fooled around. I let her know because I didn't want somebody else to tell her.

If I got pregnant I wouldn't get an abortion. The reason why is because I feel it is killing. I feel this way – if the woman and the man were old enough, understanding what they were doing, then she should have the baby. You don't go and tell me that a person like Terry, the girl I take care of for Mrs Mack, if she had sex, she didn't know what she was doing – she certainly would. She hasn't had any sex, but say she did, you can't tell me just because she is partially mongoloid that she didn't understand. If the person that is having sex knows what they are doing – and most of them do, or they wouldn't do it – even if they don't understand, they do it because it is love and it is warmness. I feel that if they are able to do it they understand what is going to happen after and shouldn't get an abortion. They should not have did it in the first place.

It's like they should have the whole thing – the pains and everything – because then it would teach them to realize that it is not just having all this fun, but is the pain of delivery and everything. They will realize the next time. They will run as fast as they can go.

After you have the baby you should be able to keep it if you want. I don't care, even if you are in the school, you should be able to. You shouldn't have to adopt it out like a lot of them do. They might adopt it out for a while to give it a nice home, but when they get out they should be able to have it back. They should be able to see their child any time they want to.

Now there are some people that are not even able to understand, not able to take care of themselves. Now that's different. If they got pregnant and someone just used them, then they could have an abortion. When I was talking about not having an abortion, I was speaking in terms of people like me or close to me. People that have a brain and know what they are doing.

Yesterday I was with Mrs Mack. She keeps asking me about when I am moving in. I told her I wasn't feeling good. I told her to stop pressuring me and leave me alone. I was really upset. She wanted to stay and she kept adding on. I didn't like that so I said, 'Why don't you get yourself in gear and go home?' She said, 'Pat, you know that I really care. I love you.' I just want her to understand that things don't happen overnight. It's really pressuring me right now. I am really worried about it. I told her to go. She came back at 7:00 and she knelt down by me and said, 'Are you all right?' and I said, 'Yeah, I am feeling better now.' She came back and said that she cared. I thought, 'All you care about is my money.' I didn't say that, but that's how I felt inside.

I start out in a new place great and then, after I get to know people, it falls apart. I can't understand to this day why this happens. Even now, when I spend a long time living with people, it's the same. Like with Mrs Mack. I think it is because I'm nervous about leaving my own place and my privacy and having to go and live with another family again. She said to me, 'Pat, if that is the way you feel – if you are really going to be unhappy.' I started to cry because it was the truth and yet I was feeling bad. I didn't want to leave and yet I am a young girl and young people like to get out and go places. I don't have a car. I have to go when they get ready to go. I won't be able to have any friends. She says I will have friends. I will be able to bring them down – they can visit. But car-wise and getting out – that is the problem. I am just going to have to save money so I can get a car. Her place is in the country.

I couldn't find anybody in the city because everybody has kids that come home from college. They got to save the room. Joshua, he said he would like to help me pay rent if I wanted my own place, but that kind of didn't dig me very good. I figure, this way, he might leave any day. He could leave me flat after I start depending on his income. When you got a place you pay quite a bit. I don't know how to think about it. I start thinking that this year, maybe it won't happen. That this time I'm going to have a boyfriend longer than the other times. Like when I was in Central City. When things start getting hot and heavy maybe it will change over to marriage. Who knows? So I don't know.

Reflections

It is hard to say what retardation means to me. When someone calls me that, it's like saying I can't do anything – I am dumb, I am stupid. You are not able to be normal like other people. You can't do school work.

I knew people at the state school that were mongoloid. I never really got to be friends with any of them. They were mostly on a different ward. I would never sit down and talk to them. There was a little girl – I think her name was Janice – she was on my ward. I used to talk with her, but she would jibber. Her tongue was long and she couldn't talk hardly. You couldn't sit down and have a conversation with her because you couldn't understand what she had to say. It didn't bother me though.

A lot of people on the outside would run and poke fun at retarded people. They do that down at the school I am going to now. There is a girl there that is going with a funny-looking guy. His nose is way out and his lips are funny. He was born that way. People just stare and poke fun at him right in front of his face. They laugh at him. I can't see that. I'm in their class. It is an elementary school in the day, but it is high school for us. I don't think that is right. I get very angry – inside I just turn around. I don't think anybody should poke fun at anybody else.

People make fun because they just want to put on a show. They want to act cute or better than other people. It's like, 'Look at me.' But when you get in the position of being the person they are making fun of, it's different. That's why I won't poke fun at anybody. I have lived with that. I understand that if I had somebody poke fun at me I wouldn't like it.

People don't make fun of me because I don't do anything to make them do anything. I don't look like there is anything wrong with me. Sometimes I open my big mouth and start telling people what has happened to me in my life – that I was in a state school for the retarded. That's gonna make them laugh. Now, not all people are going to. Like the church people, they are very concerned, but I'm talking about telling it to people that don't understand. Like you tell somebody about the state school and they would think that there was a reason that you were there – that there was something wrong – that there was some reason that you were there. To me, that is just nonsense, because it didn't have anything to do with the way I was. I was normal – a normal girl. But you tell somebody else that doesn't understand and you got a different thing.

Sometimes when I get upset – angry at somebody – and do things, they say, 'Well, that is why you were in the school –

because you are stupid.' The reason I act like that is because I'm mad.

I hide what happens to me from those kind of people. I know that if I tell some people, they would spread it around. It's hard because you don't know who can hold it in to themselves.

At the state school everyone knew. So, like, I would get angry or upset. Maybe the work or school wasn't going right and I would blurt out. They would say that that was the reason I was there, because I am not able to think for myself before I blurt out. They would say I was retarded or something. The worst word that I hate to be called is retarded. That's because I am not retarded. Anyone that says that doesn't understand the way I can carry myself and understand myself and take care of myself. I don't call anybody retarded that can do that. I might call that needing professional help, but I wouldn't say she was retarded.

When they told me Mary Jo was retarded – boy! – did I ever get furious. I said that she is not retarded. 'I don't want to hear it again. She has problems, she needs help, but she is not retarded.' When that girl told me that, I got right up and smashed her. I don't like that.

You tell people you have been in the state school and they think I am retarded. People go by the school and they see some of the people walking around and they think that everybody is retarded. I would be sitting on the wall and people would be coming by and say, 'Who's up there, are they all retarded? Are you retarded?' 'No, I am not retarded.' I didn't think about it then. It was really weird looking when they had those old buildings up there. We would tell them that all the people up there weren't stupid acting. It was after I got out of the school that the word retarded started to bother me.

At Empire we had quite a lot of people like me. There was so many like me and so many like them. At Cornerstone State School there were more like them. A lot of the kids just weren't able to study like we were, or go out to work, but some could dress themselves and feed themselves. Some could understand but couldn't put it into action. Some could speak. Like, you would say, 'Go over there and get that piece of paper,' and they would go right over there and get it. To me that is understanding, even if they couldn't dress themselves. Their understanding was fine. Some were not capable of going and doing things. Not enough people took the time to help them – to show them how to put on their own clothes. You can show those kind of people how to put on their clothes if they can understand and can feed themselves. There was some that couldn't dress or eat – they couldn't do anything but sit and rock and watch TV. They didn't even understand that they were watching. They would sit there and watch it because it was something. There were very smart people like me. They understood things about the world. A lot of them said that they were dumped there by their parents. They didn't want no part of them. They couldn't get rid of them any other way but throw them somewhere.

One time I wanted to see my records. I just wanted to see them because I would like to find out how I was. What I did. Why I was put in so many places instead of a regular home. I wanted to see them because maybe there is something that I don't even know about. I tried to see them, but they wouldn't let me. They said, 'Pat, oh you wouldn't want that. We already asked the doctor and he thought it would not be good.' The doctors don't have any right to make up my mind about how I feel about seeing my records. What I was three or four years ago doesn't mean what I am going to be now. Now, if they let me see the records when I was, say, sixteen or fifteen, I would probably have gone berserk over them. I wasn't stable enough in my mind yet. I wasn't ready to settle down to realize that happened.

Here I am twenty years old. At Empire State School they put me in straitjackets, in dark closets, and made me scrub stairs and the bathroom. Those kinds of things, even now, are built up inside. All this anger going through my mind – why me? Why me, locked up in a stupid place like that? I look back into my past and say, 'Pat, look at those things you went through and now look at all you can do. Why did you have to go through what you went through? Why did you have to go to Empire and Cornerstone? Why did I have to go through that cruelty?' It really disturbs me. It makes me upset in my mind, in my body, everywhere. It is an awful feeling.

I remember one day I came home from work and sat down on the couch, right here, and I just burst out crying. I didn't have anything to cry about. But the tears just came. Nobody was here. I just closed the curtains and shut everything up and cried. I just feel that I wanted to be in the dark, all closed in. I can't give an explanation why I felt like that, and that wasn't the first time. Just everything goes through my mind. I remember about Empire and Cornerstone.

Why did mom ever say, 'Pat needs professional help, she is retarded, she does things a normal girl wouldn't do?' This is what goes through my mind. Mom didn't have that much love. She had to call me retarded. I am saying that I am normal. Just because I did those things doesn't mean I am retarded. It's the things that happen in life that did it and things that they did to me when I was a baby.

3 Conclusion

Ed's and Pat's stories are unique in the literature on mental
retardation. The lives and experiences of people labeled retarded
rarely have been presented as they themselves view and understand them (see Stanovich and Stanovich, 1979). With the exception of Nigel Hunt's (1967) life story, *The World of Nigel Hunt*,
autobiographies of the so-called retarded have been unavailable.
Further, as Lorber (1974: 1) points out, except for Edgerton's *The
Cloak of Competence* (1967), 'no one has ever asked the mentally
retarded for their opinion about mental retardation.'

The reason for the scarcity of first-person accounts from those
labeled mentally retarded has to do with the perspective most
researchers, scholars, and professionals bring to the study of
mental retardation. The predominant mode of research in the
field of mental retardation is characterized by the 'official' view.
That is, researchers have taken for granted the reality of the concept of mental retardation. They have assumed the existence of
what they have tried to study, rather than treating it as proble-
matic or as a matter to be investigated (Douglas, 1971). Thus,
researchers have studied the causes and consequences of mental
retardation as a pathological state: 'What causes mental retardation?' 'How many people are retarded?' 'How can mental
retardation be treated?' 'What characteristics of the retarded are
associated with successful community adjustment?'

Our approach involves suspending conventional beliefs and
assumptions in order to understand social phenomena such as
mental retardation. This means treating all views of reality as
equally valid, rather than accepting some as 'true' and others as
'false.' The perspectives of the retarded are just as valid as the
perspectives of those who study them or purport to serve them.

The illusive and relative nature of 'truth' is illustrated by our
own research on institutions for the mentally retarded (Bogdan
et al., 1974; Bogdan and Taylor, 1975; Taylor, 1978; Taylor and
Bogdan, 1980). People who manage institutions, work in them,
and live in them present contradictory pictures and perspectives
of institutional life. Explanations, descriptions, understandings,

and interpretations vary from person to person. Obviously, the views of the staff will differ from those of the residents; but also, between administrator and aide, volunteer and visitor, maintenance worker and nurse, or doctor and educator perceptions may vary dramatically. These people differ not only in their understandings of organizational goals and practices, but also in their views of each other and of mental retardation.

For example, we have heard markedly disparate explanations for institutional abuse and dehumanization. Attendants or aides may explain abuse as a form of discipline or as a response to the frustrations of their jobs. Administrators attribute abuse to 'a few rotten apples in the barrel.' Residents might view abuse in terms of mean or uncaring staff. Outside critics might look to the institutional context for an explanation of abusive behavior. Similarly, different people may hold different perspectives on institutional programs (Bogdan et al., 1974). Administrators and professionals see programs as providing solutions to chronic institutional problems such as overcrowding and understaffing. Direct-care staff tend to see programs as fads. For residents, programs simply provide a way of passing time at the institution.

The contradictions relate to people's most general interpretations of an institution. For instance, we have documented that some people can describe an institution as a 'model facility, one of the best of its kind,' while other people will describe the same institution as a 'snakepit.'

People's views of residents further exemplify the gross differences among perspectives. Some may interpret behaviors such as rocking and headbanging as a direct consequence of severe mental retardation. Others, in turn, view such behavior as a response to boredom, deprivation, and lack of programming.

When such contradictory statements emerge during observations of institutional life, who should be believed? Is there actually one perspective – perhaps that of the administrators, or the doctors, or the residents – which more accurately than all of the others reflects the reality of institutional life? Could we average out the comments of various people in the setting to arrive at a fair picture of the truth? Is there a truthful view?

In searching for some true or objective perspective, one cannot help but ask whether people lie about their experiences in the institution. Do attendants lie? Or is it the administrators who wish to deceive? And what of the residents like Ed and Pat? Do they tell the truth? People who work or live in institutions, or in any organization, for that matter, tend to hold different understandings of what they see. The now trite phrase 'Beauty is in the eye of the beholder,' perhaps most easily conveys the idea that people often see the same object, event, or occurrence differently. Not only do people describe things differently, they point to different causes and explanations. Hence the business manager and general administrator may view the facility through their persistent concern for the financial status of the institution, whereas the program director may examine the institution in terms of therapeutic needs and training programs. The residents may concern themselves with the personalities of other residents and the rules of living for each ward, while attendants might perceive the day-to-day life of the institution in terms of the custodial tasks before them. Similarly, our perspectives may simply reflect the kind of training we have experienced. Some people have undergone training in psychology and will, therefore, tend to interpret people's behavior through psychological models, while the frame of reference for others may be the social meaning of retardation.

Truth then emerges not as one objective view or perspective, but rather as the composite of how people think about the institution and each other. Truth comprises the perspectives of administrators, line-level staff, professional workers, outsiders, volunteers, maintenance staff, family, and residents. Research in mental retardation and institutions comes from people in powerful positions vis-à-vis the so-called retarded. These views may not be lies, but they do not represent the whole story either.

The stories of the powerless – the judged – add an important dimension to the study of mental retardation.

Social and Cultural Research in Mental Retardation

Our research builds on three classic studies which deal with mental retardation as a social and cultural phenomenon: Robert Edgerton's *The Cloak of Competence* (1967), Dorothea Braginsky and Benjamin Braginsky's *Hansels and Gretels* (1971), and Jane Mercer's *Labeling the Mentally Retarded* (1973). Each of these works made an important contribution to the sociological and anthropological study of mental retardation. Each was the leading edge of a new way of thinking about the retarded. Indeed, these books are widely read and accepted in professional circles today and continue to influence the field. It is a testimonial to the importance of these three works that we feel it necessary to distinguish our own from them.[1]

Like those of Edgerton, Braginsky and Braginsky, and Mercer, our 'subjects' – Ed and Pattie – have been defined as mildly retarded, rather than severely retarded. As noted in the Introduction, however, we explicitly include all persons labeled retarded in our analysis. That is to say, we deny the validity, meaningfulness, and usefulness of the concept of mental retardation as applied to any group of human beings. Indeed, those labeled 'severely and profoundly retarded' may be harmed most by the social consequences of labeling – social rejection, stereotyping, institutionalization, the self-fulfilling prophecy.

Edgerton and Mercer concern themselves mainly with the so-called mildly retarded. Thus, Edgerton's (1967: 6) main thesis is summed up as follows: 'most mental retardation is mild men-

1 We also recognize the fact that these scholars may have changed their views since these studies were published some years ago (see especially Edgerton and Bercovici, 1976). Our goal is not to criticize these scholars, but merely to counter some of the currently accepted ideas and perspectives contained in their studies.

tal retardation, and mild mental retardation is a social phenomenon through and through.' Mercer's (1973) 'social system perspective' does not exclude the severely and profoundly retarded,
but they are peripheral to her discussion.

Not only do Edgerton and Mercer fail to apply their insights to
people labeled 'severely retarded,' they perpetuate conventional
myths regarding these persons as well. Edgerton (1967: 2) has
this to say: 'the term mental retardation applies to persons who
are so profoundly physically disabled and intellectually enfeebled
that they must spend their entire lives lying inert in cribs where
they are literally able to do nothing more than vegetate.' Mercer
(1973: 197) characterizes labeling as positive for some:

There are those who are protected by the label of mental retardate
because they cannot manage their own affairs. They need nurturance
and supervision. There are others for whom the label retardate is a
burden and a stigma, depriving them of an opportunity for a full education and plaguing them as they strive to find a place for themselves in
adult society. A critical issue in mental retardation is that of distin-
guishing those for whom the label is a shield from those for whom it is
an impediment.

While Edgerton and Mercer document the devastating effects of
labeling, they do not challenge the concept of mental retardation. They simply conclude that the cut-off point between 'them'
and 'us' should be moved.

Braginsky and Braginsky (1971) offer contradictory views on
the so-called severely disabled. *Hansels and Gretels* is clearly a
book about the experiences of the mildly retarded, whom the
Braginskys variously describe as 'educable,' 'cultural-familial,'
and 'unknown-origin.' At the very beginning of their book, they
state that they are specifically concerned with the mildly retarded.
In passing, Braginsky and Braginsky (1971: 11) offer some dispar-
aging views of the so-called profoundly retarded: 'One's pity for
the profoundly retarded is tempered somehow by the obvious

nature of their defects, and one is relieved that institutions exist which assume this human burden.'

In contrast to Edgerton and Mercer, however, the Braginskys, toward the end of their book, directly attack the concept of mental retardation as applied to the profoundly retarded. Braginsky and Braginsky (1971: 179) write: 'There is no reason, however, to assume that mental retardation is a relevant concept even for brain-damaged children. That is, we believe that here too the concept serves only to distort and obfuscate the meaning of the actual disability.' Unfortunately, after providing this insight, the authors proceed to offer a narrow and negative view of these children: 'Moreover, it is ludicrous to use the label "mental retardate" for the profoundly brain-damaged child who cannot function at all on any psychological or physiological level. For example, one would hardly label a man in a comatose state "mentally retarded" because he cannot function intelligently.' In concluding their study, the Braginskys go further than Mercer or Edgerton by applying their proposed reforms to all people labeled retarded.

Ed's and Pattie's stories will remind most people of Edgerton's study (1967), rather than Mercer's (1973) or Braginsky and Braginsky's (1971). Mercer and the Braginskys use a different methodological approach (although the Braginskys also include some good first-person accounts) and focus respectively on schools and institutions. Like our own study, Edgerton's *The Cloak of Competence* deals with the experience of being defined as mentally retarded. Specifically, he explores stigma among the mildly mentally retarded. For this reason, we devote the following pages to Edgerton's work.

Based on data collected in the early 1960s, Robert Edgerton's book drew upon in-depth interviews and participant observation conducted among forty-eight 'ex-patients' of a California institution ('hospital') for the mentally retarded. As stated at the beginning of the book, Edgerton's (1967: 7) goal was similar to ours – to collect former residents' own stories, to see their experiences through their own eyes, and to understand their thoughts and emotions. We want to spend some time discussing his book, for, although it seems quite similar to ours, the two are very different. The differences relate to theoretical assumptions about 'retardation' and 'truth.'

His goal to view the ex-residents through their own eyes notwithstanding, Edgerton studies his subjects from a traditional – official – perspective. His analysis begins with detailed portraits of four persons. His subjects do not tell their stories in their own words. Edgerton paints the picture of what they are like and how they see themselves. While he presents these portraits as objective accounts, Edgerton fails to deal with the issue of 'truth' – whose truth should the researcher accept? The portraits are based on case records as well as interviews with ex-residents, their family members, and their friends. Edgerton often presents the ex-residents from an official perspective; that is, through the eyes of institutional administrators, professionals, and other staff. The following is Edgerton's account of the events in one man's life: 'he became increasingly disturbed, with episodes of dangerously aggressive behavior. For example, at age eight, he strangled another little boy and only artificial respiration saved the victim's life ... He was regularly reported to be a behavior problem for fighting, masturbation, and voyeurism, and eventually his behavior became completely unacceptable.' For Edgerton, case record entries are 'facts,' while ex-residents' accounts are fabrications or rationalizations.

The remainder of *The Cloak of Competence* deals with the lives of the forty-eight ex-residents. Edgerton reports that the ex-residents disliked institutionalization. They recount incidents of abuse and dehumanization – exploitation, forced labor, involuntary sterilization (forty-four of the forty-eight ex-residents had been sterilized). Many ex-residents believed that their institutionalization had been debilitating and hindered them in adjusting to life on the outside.

Edgerton does not accept the ex-residents' definition of the institution as a depriving environment at face value. On the contrary, he depicts ex-residents' accounts as a symptom of their inability to deal with their mental retardation. For example, he quotes one resident's comments on the institution:

Lots of the patients in that hospital are smarter than the people outside. The problem is that when you have been locked away in there for a long time you get nervous and also you don't learn how to live outside, so when you get outside you can't act like a normal person – even when you are smarter than outside people. I was there so long I thought I was going to rot. It's not right. I never belonged there and they kept me so long that now I'm confused and nervous and can't get a job. (1967: 71)

Edgerton then offers the following commentary on this person's reflections: 'And so the excuse continues, for as long as anyone will listen.' Elsewhere, he comments, 'Today the many excellent institutions for the mentally retarded are staffed by competent and sympathetic professionals' (1967: 210). Clearly, he accepts official views over those of ex-residents.

Edgerton analyzes residents' accounts of why they were first admitted to the state facility. He assumes that the real reason they were admitted is because they *are* 'mentally retarded' and, therefore, incompetent. The reasons that *they* give for being admitted are treated as lies or fabrications. As he puts it:

One of the first needs of the ex-patients was concealment of their institutional history, a past which, if revealed, could be gravely discrediting. This concealment was regularly attempted through a stereotyped tale which explained and excused their confinement in the hospital by revealing the 'real' reason they were there. Such excuses were collected from all the forty-eight ex-patients. The excuses fell into nine categories. (1967: 148)

The most commonly given 'excuse' was abandonment by a parent or relative.[2] One must ask why he treats these as excuses, and

---

2 In contrast to Edgerton, Goffman (1961) presents such statements as understandable reactions to institutional inmates' situations.

why he is satisfied that 'mental retardation' is the reason for their confinement. The following summarizes his perspective on his subjects: 'By attributing their relative incompetence to the depriving experience of institutionalization, and by insisting that the institutionalization was unjustified, the ex-patients have an available excuse that can and does sustain self esteem' (1967: 170). He interprets the ex-patients' perspectives in the framework of his and the administration's belief in 'mental retardation.'

Edgerton approaches the ex-residents with certain assumptions. In discussing his sample, he suggests that he believed they were incompetent when he was in search of them; 'Such a population of incompetent persons was available' (Edgerton, 1967: 19). He had preconceived notions about how a 'retarded' person should act and look:

There is nothing in his appearance to suggest that he is anything less than a normal man, and his speech is likewise unexceptionable ... To the casual observer, he is an ordinary man ... (1967: 45).

His speech is clear and his vocabulary surprisingly good ... The impression generally is of a sullen suspicious rustic man, but not necessarily a retarded one (1967: 25).

The overall first impression is that of a not very well educated, 'scatterbrained' housewife, but not necessarily a mentally retarded one (1967: 81).

Edgerton's basic thesis is that the incompetence of the mentally retarded is stigmatizing; that is, destructive of their self-esteem. In Edgerton's (1967: 207) words: 'For all of these persons, an admission of mental retardation is unacceptable – totally and without exception ... the ex-patients explain neither their past institutional confinement nor their current incompetence in the community in terms of their own stupidity. They employ almost any other excuse ... Never is mental retardation admitted.' Edgerton sympathizes with the stigma of the ex-patients and even suggests that a new word be created to describe mild mental retardation. However, he concludes by accepting the brutal effects of stigma as inevitable since 'societies cannot fail to be concerned with the incompetence of their members' (1967: 218).

For Edgerton, the retarded are basically incompetent. Their words are not to be taken seriously. They spend a good deal of their time and energy trying to hide their retardation by pretending to be competent; hence, the title, *The Cloak of Competence*. As Edgerton (1967: 218) states: 'In a sense, these retarded persons are like the emperor in the fairy tale who thought he was wearing the most elegant garments but in fact was wearing nothing at all.'

The Judged

Our approach to studying mental retardation has differed from those of previous researchers in the field. We have not assumed the validity of the concept of mental retardation. We resist the tendency to think that, because certain people are called retarded, 'retardation' must be an entity having an independent existence. We approached our subjects with skepticism, not about them, but about what they had been called. We did not assume that their utterances were symptoms of 'retardation.'

Like the people in Edgerton's study, Ed and Pat view 'retarded' as a demeaning, stigmatizing label. As Ed states: 'I never thought of myself as a retarded individual ... I never really had that ugly feeling down deep.' And in Pat's words: 'The worst word that I hate to be called is retarded. That's because I am not retarded.'

Like Edgerton's subjects, Ed and Pat do not define themselves as retarded. This is not surprising, for, as Ed puts it, 'Who would want to?' Indeed, why would they want to be associated with a category for which they and others have so much disdain?

Since they do not accept the label 'retarded,' how do they explain their treatment by others, especially their confinement in an institution for the mentally retarded? It is not that they deny having had their share of problems. Pattie believes that she is 'disturbed' and even, at times, toys with the idea, given to her by her mother, that she was mentally damaged when her father threw her against a wall as a child. Ed thinks of himself as being handicapped in some ways – for example, in not being able to think as well as others at certain times – but he also thinks of himself as having struggled with and largely overcome his deficiencies. While they acknowledge their problems, they do not see these as the reasons they were sent to an institution for the mentally retarded. Both see their placement in terms of a lack of alternatives. They see themselves as having suffered from contingencies: crisis, weakness in the family, and particular personal difficulties at crucial times in their lives. They do realize that their IQs made them eligible for admission, but they see neither their test scores nor retardation as having been central to their institutionalization.

If we had not spent so much time listening to Ed and Pattie and had not approached our research with skepticism regarding the concept of retardation, we might have talked about their understandings of their institutional confinement as 'cover stories' – as the way they protect themselves from dealing with their 'real' problem, mental retardation. But from their point of view, retardation is the cover story. It is the way officials and professionals account for their own treatment of people.

Ed's and Pattie's official records paint a picture that is dramatically different from their own accounts of what they are like and what they have experienced. These records present their reactions to their situations as pathological, rather than as natural and normal responses to depriving environments and dehumanizing experiences. For instance, Ed's records depict him as 'a nice boy, but easily confused.' Pattie's records are filled with references to her as 'depressed,' 'angry,' 'quick-tempered,' and 'preoccupied with personal difficulties.' A relatively recent psychological report concludes that she has 'a verbal problem,' and is 'highly self-absorbed, an afflicted adolescent girl who alternately overcontrols her strong emotions.'

What, then, is the 'truth' about Ed and Pattie? Our previous discussion reveals our own attitude to that question. The truth of Ed's and Pat's condition cannot be explained by deferring to official definitions of their problems. Their compelling words require that we give them at least as much credence as we do their judges.

It is important to note that Ed and Pat not only deny the applicability of the label 'retarded' to themselves, but state that there are many people in state schools who, as they put it, are as smart as they. These others, like themselves, are seen as being there because no one wants them or can maintain them in their homes. There is ambiguity on their part about whom the label should be applied to, if anyone. Both agree that the term is a bad one to use when talking about anybody, yet on occasion they use it, or similar terms, when describing others at the institution. Their use of the label is confined to people who have severely impaired physical functioning and who do not communicate verbally, and is used synonymously with the conventional institutional term 'low grade.' For Ed and Pat, if the term 'retarded' has to be used, it should be reserved for these people whom they see as unable to care for their own physical needs.

A different interpretation of Ed and Pat's understanding of 'retardation' is emerging, different from the one presented by Edgerton. As we have already illustrated, he and others suggest that we should understand that when people who are labeled retarded do not agree with their designation, they are denying the reality of their being – that they can't face the truth of their condition. This view is based on the premise – the official view – that everyone in an institution or anyone below a certain test score is objectively retarded – that retardation itself is a fact. Ed and Pat are saying something more profound – at least, to those who can regard their denial that they are 'retarded' as more than just a defense mechanism. Essentially, their claim is not that they personally have been misdiagnosed 'retarded' but that the system that is used to classify people as either 'retarded' or 'normal' is wrong and misleading. It is erroneous to classify people as 'retarded' because it does not produce the kinds of services that it is in their best interests to receive. Moreover, having lived among the 'retarded' and been so labeled themselves, they have come to look for and see the intelligence in themselves and in their friends, not the 'retardation.' They have come to understand that the picture painted by the name 'retardate' is a caricature. It is not that they don't see their situation as it really is. They have a different view of it from those who have judged them – they have a 'truth' generated from a different place in the service delivery system.

In their struggle not to be called 'retarded,' those so labeled are often powerless. Their competing view of retardation is not treated seriously either by those with whom they come in contact or in the literature on retardation.

Ed and Pat have limited influence on the way others define the reality of their situation for a number of reasons. The strength of received opinion about concepts like 'mental retardation' is one. As their stories suggest, there is a dearth of definitions in our society. Few agencies acknowledge that individuals who are mentally and physically different need positive ways of conceptualizing themselves, with the result that more dignified alternatives to the demeaning vocabulary of 'sick,' 'handicapped,' 'deviant,' and 'retardate' have not been actively sought. In addition, the label of retardation is a master status – that is, once the label is attached to you, it determines how others relate to you. It is stigmatizing; it tells the world that you don't measure up. If professionals with their elaborate vocabulary, tests, and rituals decree that an individual is retarded, what is the chance that a denial by the judged would be seriously considered? As Ed tells us: 'It really doesn't help a person's character the way the system treats you. One thing that's hard is that once you're in it, you can't convince them how smart you are ... you're so weak you can't really fight back.'

Being processed by the 'retardation' delivery system promotes this inability to fight back. Not only do the so-called retarded bear the stigma of the label, they are also put at a disadvantage by it when attempting to combat its negative effects. There is no need to go through the details of their experience, an experience that most likely parallels that of countless other labeled people. Ed gives us a sense of what it means when he says: 'You lose so much. They take the human character – you've heard of raping a girl – they rape the character until by the time you get in, you feel so low you don't know what's happening. Then one day you wake up and you say, "What the fuck am I doing here?" It tears you down.'

Pattie captures the confusion of admission to the state school with her comments:

I was thinking, 'Why am I here?' ... I saw some people that looked like me, but I remember saying to myself, 'What am I doing here? I don't deserve to be here. I don't have any problems.' I talked to someone and asked her why I was there and she told me that I was there because they felt I needed to be.

With all those people dressed in white uniforms, and the beds white, and the towels white, I felt like I was in a hospital. It wasn't anything like a school. I started thinking that something happened to me or something. I thought that maybe I had gotten sick and I had to be in the hospital for that. I thought that maybe I needed help to get better.

The degradation ceremonies and identity-stripping (Garfinkel, 1956; Goffman, 1961) that are part of admission to an institution are well-illustrated in Ed and Pat's stories. Being stripped of their clothes, privacy, and possessions of the past makes them particularly vulnerable to being cast in a variety of institutional roles, such as: baby, patient, prisoner, wild one, jester, vegetable, low grade, and animal. Humiliation, straitjackets, dirty work, disease, and parasites were part of the experiences of Ed and Pat as children. While their stories are testimonials to the ability of human beings to survive the systematic and brutal attack on the self, they also reveal that such attacks leave scars, even on the strongest of the subjected. Pat and Ed's reflections on the present reveal self-concepts that have been shaken. While they do not define their 'selves' as retarded, there are traces of gnawing doubts about themselves in their thoughts. Ed reveals this when he says: 'The whole idea of having been in a state school makes you nervous about why you were ever put there in the first place.' Talking about her visits home from the state school, Pat reveals similar doubts about herself: 'I felt abnormal because I wasn't living with my family. I felt abnormal because I was at the state school. I felt abnormal – like I wouldn't play with the other kids and go outside for walks. I didn't feel like I was crazy – just abnormal.'

Not only has their bout in the state-school shaken their self-concepts, but it also has deprived them of the opportunity to learn the social skills that are necessary to survive unnoticed in the world outside the institution. Further, they learned ways of behaving that were actually detrimental to their taking up life in the larger world. As Ed puts it: 'Living in Empire was not like growing up.' The routines of the institution deny them the chance of becoming independent and self-sufficient. The system of allocating clothing and food deprives them of the opportunity to learn how and what to buy. The mass showering and grooming keeps them from developing personal hygiene habits.

Pat and Ed's stories are ones of lost opportunity brought about by institutional confinement. For years they lived in an upside-down world where you lined up and did what you were told, or suffered immediate and often brutal consequences. It was a world in which boys and girls, men and women were segregated from each other and where there was prolonged discouragement of love and caring. There is strong evidence in their stories to suggest that their experience in the state school made them less competent than they might have been if they hadn't gone there.

Their accounts of leaving the institution and their present life show the effects their institutional heritage has had on them. Having to learn about the basics of independent living from scratch, about the world of work, about dealing with being alone – these all had to be faced. As Ed puts it:

Nobody ever told me I had to work and nobody told me I had to fill out a bank form. If you have never had to face them – wow, it's a brand-new world ... When you leave a state school, one of the things you really miss is the people. You also find that the world is bigger than you are used to having it. The one thing you find is loneliness.

Reflecting on the lack of basic skills an ex-institutionalized person has, Pat says: 'The major problem with people leaving the state school is that you are so used to everything being handed to you. Like your food is provided, and you don't have to cook. You don't know how to do your laundry. They do it for you ... When you get out, it is no fun because you don't know what the outside is all about.' The heterosexual world is also strange to Pattie and Ed. One can understand some of their problems of heterosexual adjustment not in terms of 'retarda-tion' but as manifestations of institutional deprivation. Ed's fumbling at taking someone to the movies and Pat's succession of lovers have their roots in the sex-segregated institutional model.

While we have emphasized thus far the difficulties involved in Ed and Pat's leaving the institution and being on their own, we must not ignore the benefits. After all, neither Ed nor Pat want to go back. They appreciate the things many of us take for granted – the plain joy of freedom and independence; having no one to answer to but yourself; having privacy; doing simple house-hold-management tasks like laundry and shopping; spending

money; travelling; dressing up; going on trips; getting a paycheck; meeting new people; being self-sufficient; taking risks;
getting drunk; sleeping in; staying up.

The troubles that Ed and Pattie faced leaving the institution
were only part of their problem. While learning to live in a non-
institutional world had its difficulties, these could be conquered
in a short period of time. What was less easy to conquer was the
stigma of the state school. While they do not define themselves
as retarded and thus can save themselves the humiliation of that
label, there is no way that they can deny having been residents
of a state school for the mentally retarded. As our previous discussion revealed, they understand that they were not sent to the
state school because they were retarded, but others will not
believe it. They learn that, for most, having been a resident of
an institution is synonymous in people's minds with being
'retarded' or 'crazy.' Pat suggests some of the dilemmas of being
a former resident when she comments:

When I was working at these places, I usually made a big mistake. You
can make friends by telling people a little about your life. Well, I made
enemies by telling them about mine ... They started burning you, so I
just don't talk about it to anybody ... It's hard. Like, people will ask you,
'Where were you a couple of years ago?' I can't say Timbuktu or Ohio
when I was never there ... When you look for a job, they ask, 'What
kind of a job did you hold? Where did you live?' and things like
that ... They say that is the reason that you get upset, because you was
in a school with retarded and crazy people.

Everybody thinks that Cornerstone is for really crazy people. That
really hurts. I tell them that there are people there that need more help
than others, but it doesn't sink in.

The institution has been a significant part of their lives, yet they
cannot share that experience with others for fear of having it
turned back on them, for fear that it will cause people to define
them in a way they don't want to be defined. At the same time,

there is a need to share the deprivation of their institutional lives with others. They want to hide their past, but how do they hide years of their lives in a society in which people must have pasts? They want to share their suffering, but the price may be the humiliation of being categorized.

The salience of the institution in these people's lives – its negative effects on the self and on socialization, and the stigma of being associated with it – suggests that these people have been victimized by the hoax that is a cure for the imaginary disease known as retardation. The system of delivering services and the label of 'retardation' have indeed covered Ed and Pattie with a cloak, a cloak of incompetence.

A Final Note

The label 'mentally retarded' creates barriers to our understanding people on their own terms. It prevents us from seeing and treating the people so defined as human beings with feelings, understandings, and needs. When we label people, we lose the ability to empathize with them – to see the world from their point of view.

Ed Murphy and Pattie Burt are articulate and reflective persons. Reading about their experiences, one cannot help but be outraged at how they have been defined and treated. Ironically, few professionals and researchers in the field of mental retardation today would defend their incarceration in state schools or developmental centers, or the dehumanizing treatment they have received at the hands of the many social-service agencies with which they have been involved. 'Deinstitutionalization' and 'normalization' for the mildly retarded have become widely accepted over the past decade.

The lessons to be learned from Ed and Pat's stories apply to all those we have called 'mentally retarded.' Though our narrators may be better able to express themselves than many persons

labeled retarded, what they have to say tells us at least as much **223**
about our society and the debilitating effects of labeling as it does
about the speakers.

The field of mental retardation currently is embroiled in a
deep and bitter controversy over whether the so-called severely
and profoundly retarded should live among their fellow human
beings (see Center on Human Policy, 1979). As a reaction to the
moral and ideological arguments of the deinstitutionalization (or,
more precisely, anti-institutionalization) movement, researchers
and professionals have demanded 'empirical' (by which they
mean quantified psychological variables) evidence that the severely disabled should live in communities, rather than in institutions (Edgerton et al., 1975; Zigler, 1977; Partlow Review
Committee, 1979).

What kind of evidence is needed to determine that the so-
called retarded should not be cast out from society and subjected
to living conditions other persons would not tolerate? One need
only set aside the labels and preconceived notions and empathize with those labeled mentally retarded to find all the evidence necessary. Ed Murphy tells us this when he describes his
friend, Tommy McCan: 'Tommy was a guy who was really nice
to be with. You could sit down with him and have a nice conversation and enjoy yourself. He was a mongoloid. The trouble was,
people couldn't see beyond that. If he didn't look that way it
would have been different, but there he was locked into what the
other people thought he was.'

Recently we visited a house in which six former residents of
a large state institution lived. The house was well-staffed and
the residents were involved in activities and in the day-to-day
operation of the house. It was less expensive to maintain these
people at the house than at the state institution. These had been
considered to be the 'most violent,' the 'most aggressive,' the
'hardest to manage' at the institution. They were what institutional staff and professionals had defined as the 'worst cases.'
These were not the 'cream puffs.' None of them had well-deve-

loped verbal skills and three could not speak at all. One had broken windows in the institution, another had stabbed people, another had been in a constant state of screaming rage and self-mutilation. After three months in an environment that empha-sized their humanness, these people had changed dramatically. We visited the bleak wards where they had lived prior to their involvement in this new experimental living arrangement. We heard testimony from staff of how 'bad' they had been and how they had changed. These people were certainly not 'cured' in a clinical sense, but they were no longer occupying the station in life that had been imposed upon them previously. They were different because they had been placed in an environment that expected change, that didn't define their problem as 'retardation' or any innate condition, but rather defined them as people who could live and grow. They had managed to break out of the cycle of deprivation followed by deterioration followed by further deprivation. They were called by their real names, not by their diagnosis and they were responding. Positive expectations, not vocabularies that provide explanations for failure, make positive change occur.

Our society and service systems are structured in such a way as to stigmatize people with obvious differences and to pose for-midable obstacles to their participation as full members. People with limited reading and writing skills are denied full access to public facilities and services. Employment applications, income-tax forms, bus schedules, street signs, school materials, and intelligence and achievement tests demand a level of reading proficiency that many people do not possess. Schools call chil-dren names (for example, 'mentally retarded,' 'severely emotion-ally disturbed,' 'learning disabled') to obtain additional funding for educational services. Severely disabled persons are given the option of obtaining care or living in community homes, but not both. Tests are used as a sorting mechanism to assign people their places in the pecking order.

By abandoning labels, we shift attention from the deficiencies of the person to those of the society and service systems. Thus, we cease to ask what is wrong with the person and begin to ask what kinds of environments and services we can create to be able to accommodate all persons in the society, to treat them with respect, and permit them dignity. Most important, when we abandon labels we are forced to listen to those whose perspectives we have ignored and to take what they have to say seriously.

Bibliography

Allport, G. 1942. *The Use of Personal Documents in Psychological Science*. New York: Social Science Research Council

Angell, R. 1945. 'A critical review of the development of the personal document method in sociology 1920-1940.' In L. Gottschalk, C. Kluckhohn, and R. Angell (eds) *The Use of Personal Documents in History, Anthropology, and Sociology*. New York: Social Science Research Council

Becker, H.S. 1966. 'Introduction' to C. Shaw's *The Jack Roller*. Chicago: University of Chicago Press

– (ed.). 1967. *The Other Side*. New York: Free Press

Berger, P.L., and T. Luckmann. 1967. *The Social Construction of Reality*. Garden City, NY: Doubleday

Binet, A., and T. Simon. 1916. *The Intelligence of the Feeble-minded* (trans. by E.S. Kite). Baltimore: Williams and Wilkins

Blatt, B. 1970. *Exodus from Pandemonium*. Boston: Allyn and Bacon

– 1973. *Souls in Extremis*. Boston: Allyn and Bacon

Blatt, B., and F. Kaplan. 1966. *Christmas in Purgatory*. Boston: Allyn and Bacon

Blatt, B., R. Bogdan, D. Biklen, and S. Taylor. 1977. 'From institution to community: A conversion model.' *Educational Programming for the Severely and Profoundly Handicapped*. Reston, Va.: Council for Exceptional Children

Blatt, B., J. McNally, and A. Ozolins. 1980. *The Family Papers*. New York: Longman

Blumer, H. 1969. *Symbolic Interactionism: Perspective and Method*. Englewood Cliffs, NJ: Prentice-Hall

Bogdan, R. 1974. *Being Different: The Autobiography of Jane Fry*. New York: John Wiley

– 1980. 'What does it mean when a person says, "I'm not retarded"?' *Education and Training of the Mentally Retarded* 15 (1; Feb.): 74-80

228   Bogdan R., and D. Biklen, 1977. 'Handicapism.' *Social Policy* March/
April: 14-19

Bogdan, R., and S. Taylor. 1975. *Introduction to Qualitative Research
Methods: A Phenomenological Approach to the Social Sciences*. New
York: John Wiley

– 1976. 'The judged, not the judges: An insider's view of mental
retardation.' *American Psychologist* 31(1): 47-52

Bogdan, R., S.J. Taylor, B. de Grandpre, and S. Haynes. 1974. 'Let
them eat programs: Attendants' perspectives and programming on
wards in state schools.' *Journal of Health and Social Behavior*
15 (June): 142-51

Briginsky, D., and B. Braginsky. 1971. *Hansels and Gretels*. New York:
Holt, Rinehart and Winston

Center on Human Policy. 1979. *The Community Imperative*. Syracuse,
NY: Center on Human Policy

Dexter, L.A. 1964. 'On the politics and sociology of stupidity in our
society.' In H.S. Becker (ed.) *The Other Side*. New York: Free Press

Douglas, J. 1971. *American Social Order*. New York: Free Press

Dugdale, R.L. 1910. *The Jukes*. New York: Putnam

Dybwad, G. 1974. *New Neighbors*. Washington, DC: President's Committee on Mental Retardation

Edgerton, R. 1967. *The Cloak of Competence*. Berkeley: University of
California Press

Edgerton, R., and S. Bercovici. 1976. 'The cloak of competence: Years
later.' *American Journal of Mental Deficiency* 80 (5): 485-97

Edgerton, R.B., and C.R. Edgerton. 1973. 'Becoming mentally
retarded in a Hawaiian school.' In R.K. Eyman, C.E. Meyers, and
G. Tarjan (eds) *Sociobehavioral Studies in Mental Retardation*. Washington, DC: American Association on Mental Deficiency

Edgerton, R.B., R.K. Eyman, and A.B. Silverstein. 1975. 'Mental
retardation system.' In N. Hobbs (ed.) *Issues in the Classification of
Children*. vol. II. San Francisco: Jossey-Bass

Eyman, R.K., C.E. Meyers, and G. Tarjan (eds). 1973. *Sociobehavioral
Studies in Mental Retardation*. Washington, DC: American Association on Mental Deficiency

Farber, B. 1968. *Mental Retardation: Its Social Context and Social Consequences*. Boston: Houghton Mifflin

Fernald, W.E. 1912. 'The burden of feeble-mindedness.' *Journal of
Psycho-asthenics* 17: 87-111

Garfinkel, H. 1956. 'Conditions of successful degradation ceremonies.' *American Journal of Sociology* 59 (March): 420-4

Goddard, H.H. 1910. 'Heredity of feeble-mindedness.' *American Breeders Magazine* 1: 165-78

– 1912. *The Kallikak Family*. New York: Macmillan

– 1915. 'The possibilities of research as applied to the prevention of feeble-mindedness.' Proceedings of the National Conference on Charities and Corrections 307-12

Goffman, E. 1961. *Asylums*. New York: Anchor Books

– 1963. *Stigma: Notes on the Management of Spoiled Identity*. Englewood Cliffs, NJ: Prentice-Hall

Grossman, H.J. (ed.). 1973. *Manual on Terminology and Classification in Mental Retardation*. Washington, DC: American Association on Mental Deficiency

Heber, R. (ed.). 1959. *A Manual on Terminology and Classification in Mental Retardation*. Washington, DC: American Association on Mental Deficiency

Hobbs, N. (ed.). 1975. *Issues in the Classification of Children*, vol. II. San Francisco: Jossey-Bass

Hunt, N. 1967. *The World of Nigel Hunt*. Beaconsfield, England: Darwin Finlayson, Ltd

Kanner, L. 1948. 'Feeblemindedness: Absolute, relative and apparent.' *The Nervous Child* 7: 365-97

Lorber, M. 1974. 'Consulting the mentally retarded: An approach to the definition of mental retardation by experts.' Dissertation, University of Michigan. Ann Arbor: University Microfilms

Mercer, J. 1973. *Labeling the Mentally Retarded*. Berkeley, Calif.: University of California Press

Merton, R.K. 1957. *Social Theory and Social Structure*. Glencoe, Ill.: Free Press

Mills, C.W. 1959. *The Sociological Imagination*. New York: Oxford

Muehlberger, C. 1972. 'The social-psychological experiences of adult former residents of a state school for the mentally retarded.' Dissertation, University of Michigan. Ann Arbor: University Microfilms

Partlow Review Committee. 1978. Memorandum, Wyatt *v.* Hardin, October 18

Platt, A.M. 1969. *The Child Savers*. Chicago: University of Chicago Press

President's Committee on Mental Retardation. 1969. *The Six-Hour Retarded Child*. Washington, DC: Superintendent of Documents

Rothman, D.J. 1971. *The Discovery of the Asylum*. Boston: Little, Brown

Ryan, W. 1971. *Blaming the Victim*. New York: Pantheon

Sarason, S., and J. Doris. 1969. *Psychological Problems in Mental Deficiency*. New York: Harper and Row

–   1979. *Educational Handicap, Public Policy and Social History*. New York: Free Press

Scheerenberger, R.C. 1979. *Public Residential Services for the Mentally Retarded*. Washington, DC: National Association of Superintendents of Public Facilities for the Mentally Retarded

Schrag, P., and D. Divoky. 1975. *The Myth of the Hyperactive Child*. New York: Dell

Shaw, C. 1966. *The Jack Roller*. 2nd ed. Chicago: University of Chicago Press

Stanovich, K.E., and P.J. Stanovich. 1979. 'Speaking for themselves: A bibliography of writings by mentally handicapped individuals.' *Mental Retardation* 17 (2; April): 83-6

Statistics Canada, Health Division. 1977. *Mental Health Statistics*

Szasz, T. 1970. *The Manufacture of Madness*. New York: Dell

–   1974. *The Myth of Mental Illness*. New York: Harper and Row

Taylor, S.J. 1978. *The custodians: Attendants and their work at state institutions for the mentally retarded*. Ann Arbor: University Microfilms

Taylor, S.J., and R. Bogdan. 1980. 'Defending illusions: The institution's struggle for survival.' *Human Organization* 39 (3; Fall): 209-18

Thomas, W.I., and F. Znaniecki. 1927. *The Polish Peasant in Europe and America*. New York: Knopf

Thompson, M.W. 1964. Conference remarks. *Mental Retardation in Canada – Report Federal-Provincial Conference*. Ottawa: Department of National Health and Welfare

Tredgold, R.F., and K. Soddy. 1956. *A Text-book of Mental Deficiency*. London: Bailliere Tindall

Wechsler, D. 1958. *The Measurement and Appraisal of Adult Intelligence*. Baltimore: Williams and Wilkins

Wolfensberger, W. 1972. *Normalization*. Toronto: National Institute on Mental Retardation

- 1975. *The Origin and Nature of Our Institutional Models*. Syracuse: Human Policy Press

Zigler, E. 1976. 'NICHHD appropriations for mental retardation.' New Haven, Conn: Yale University (unpublished report)

This book

was designed by

ANTJE LINGNER

of University of

Toronto

Press